BRUMBACK LIBRARY
3 3045 03159 4167
P9-CLE-482

THE *Jane Austen* GUIDE TO LIFE

Thoughtful Lessons for the Modern Woman

LORI SMITH

Guilford, Connecticut
An imprint of Globe Pequot Press

skirt!® is an attitude . . . spirited, independent, outspoken, serious, playful and irreverent, sometimes controversial, always passionate.

Illustrations by David Grant
Text design: Sheryl Kober
Project editor: Kristen Mellitt
Layout artist: Kirsten Livingston

Library of Congress Cataloging-in-Publication Data is available on file.

ISBN 978-0-7627-7381-7

Printed in the United States of America

10 9 8 7 6 5 4 3 2 1

For Mom and Dad, with love

And for my nieces—Grace, Eleanor, Alison, and Isabela—
with hopes that they will grow to love Austen

Also by Lori Smith

A Walk with Jane Austen
The Single Truth

Contents

Citations

Here is a list of the books I've referenced most often (other sources are listed in full in the endnotes), along with the abbreviations I've used when citing them. To make things easier for readers, I've listed volume and chapter numbers along with page numbers for quotes from the novels. For example, a quote from page 17, volume I, chapter VI of *Pride and Prejudice* would be listed this way: P&P, 17 (I, VI). I hope this way you'll be able to find these quotes easily even if you're reading a different edition. Should you need to translate the volume and chapter numbers to the more modern chapter numbering without volumes, check out the e-texts at www.mollands.net.

C: Austen, Jane. *Catharine and Other Writings.* Oxford: Oxford University Press, 1993.

E: Austen, Jane. *Emma.* Oxford: Oxford University Press, 2008.

FR: Le Faye, Deirdre. *Jane Austen: A Family Record* (Second Edition). Cambridge: Cambridge University Press, 2004.

Letters: Le Faye, Deirdre, ed. *Jane Austen's Letters* (Third Edition). Oxford: Oxford University Press, 1995.

Memoir: Austen-Leigh, J. E. *A Memoir of Jane Austen and Other Family Recollections.* Oxford: Oxford University Press, 2002.

MP: Austen, Jane. *Mansfield Park.* Oxford: Oxford University Press, 2003.

NA: Austen, Jane. *Northanger Abbey, Lady Susan, The Watsons and Sanditon.* Oxford: Oxford University Press, 2008.

P: Austen, Jane. *Persuasion.* Oxford: Oxford University Press, 2004.

P&P: Austen, Jane. *Pride and Prejudice.* Oxford: Oxford University Press, 2008.

S&S: Austen, Jane. *The Annotated Sense and Sensibility.* Annotated and edited by David M. Shapard. New York: Anchor Books, 2011.

Introduction

On a fresh Tuesday afternoon in the spring of 1811, Jane Austen sat down at her small table in the drawing room of the cottage she shared with her mother, sister, and their dear friend Martha Lloyd. She had played the piano first thing that morning—mostly country tunes—and, after breakfast with her family, worked on her needlepoint and entertained a few visitors. And now the afternoon was hers. She worked on her novel at the small wooden writing desk her father had given her. He had been the first person to try to have Jane's work published, only to receive a standard rejection from the publisher, who didn't even read the novel. Inside the writing desk were hundreds of tiny sheets, covered in script, now crossed out and written over in places.

Jane was playing with her characters from *First Impressions:* Elizabeth Bennet and Fitzwilliam Darcy. She was carefully editing the story—the one her father had sent in, the one that had been summarily rejected—with thoughts of it being published. Truthfully, with thoughts of it being ridiculously successful, though she was also a realist, and would have been content simply to have it published even if she had to pay for it out of her own pocket, so long as she didn't go into debt in the process.

So she fiddled with characters and scenes, working with her tiny scraps of paper, listening for the servants and for anyone who might come to the door, so she could quickly hide her secret project. No one outside of her family and close friends was to know that Jane Austen was a writer. While she wrote, she looked out the broad drawing room window at the comings and goings of Chawton, their tiny village in the English countryside Jane loved so dearly.

Jane Austen lived an astonishingly quiet life. She lived with her family, had a few close friends, and rarely ventured into society. Her clothes were something less than fashionable, and the cap she wore for her afternoon of writing—the kind of cap reserved for middle-aged spinsters—was plenty proof of that. She never had a lot of money; her eventual success didn't provide her even enough to live on. And while her family loved her writing, her path to publication was far from easy.

She was the youngest sister, the second youngest child in a family of eight. No one expected anything of her, except that she watch her nieces and nephews when they needed her to. And she did—she loved them.

Ironically, for all the love stories she gave us (but they're so much more than that, aren't they?), she never married.

How surprised she would be today to find that not only does her name survive, but also that she is loved and adored by women of all ages who have read her books or seen the movies that have grown out of them. This simple, unfashionable, shy, poor, country spinster has become our patron saint of romance, our goddess of happy endings. Her name is synonymous with romantic sighs, period costumes, and the ideal of what love should be. What would she think of that? And what would she think of us?

If Jane Austen could give us advice about life and love, what would she tell us?

Of course, as a woman who lived her whole life during the reign of George III, Jane could not be expected to understand tweeting or texting or platform heels (or really much about fashion, even during her own day). But as she showed herself to be such an astute student of human nature, she could teach us an awful lot about ourselves.

We are obsessed with fame. Austen didn't even want her name to be known. We dream of finding "the one." She might quibble with our wholehearted devotion to that idea. We want money and more money (or, at least our "Real Housewives" do—I think Jane would find great comic potential in that show, by the way). Jane was content to have just enough.

Like her novels, Jane's own life story translates surprisingly well into the twenty-first century. No one expected anything of her, but she pursued her dream anyway, to astounding success. Although she didn't marry, she clearly understood love. She endured some incredibly painful experiences—such as the disease that eventually took her life at the young age of forty-one—with grace and humor. She always approached life with irrepressible joy.

This book mines Jane's life and her stories for the lessons she would teach us if she could. Thankfully, through her writing, she can and does still speak today.

Chapter 1

Living Your Dreams

Jane Austen lived during an age when women were neither expected nor allowed to work, when novels were thought to be frivolous, and when women who put their names on books were considered vulgar. How strange, then, that she worked, she wrote novels, and her name survives on her books (albeit against her will—we'll get to that later). Truthfully, her name more than survives. From nearly two hundred years beyond the grave, Jane Austen is a force to be reckoned with in the entertainment industry. Movies, books, miniseries—Jane Austen lives on because she did one simple and revolutionary thing: She picked up her pen and told stories.

Many things in Austen's life are a mystery to us. She didn't keep any kind of journal that we know of. And after Jane died, her sister Cassandra burned many of Jane's letters or cut out the juiciest parts (or those that may have implicated one family member or another). Cassandra had Jane's back and made sure that nothing with a whiff of scandal or intrigue remained. But amidst the murkiness, we know one thing: Jane Austen dreamt of being a writer, and in spite of whatever roadblocks society threw in her way, she followed that dream. How very twenty-first century of her.

Austen grew up loving stories. In Jane's own words, she and her family members were all "great Novel-readers & not ashamed of being so."[1] They read together in the evenings. Her older brothers put on theatricals in the barn for family and friends, and probably let their littlest sister take small roles. She had full access to her father's large library of five hundred books and read voraciously for someone not required to by a strict schoolmaster. She knew the poetry of the era, read Henry Fielding and Samuel Richardson, devoured history and best sellers alike. She studied French and Italian and even picked up a little Latin from her brothers, who were taught the classics. Jane's quick mind loved to read and loved to learn.

It's hard to believe that the English novel ever had a beginning, that there was ever a time when novels didn't exist, but such is the case. Books were things of truth, about thoughts and ideas, or about the real lives of real people. Not until 1719, roughly fifty years before Jane was born, did books take on another form. With the publication of *Robinson Crusoe,* Daniel Defoe introduced a new kind of book: a book that told made-up stories. Suddenly, books could be whimsical and fantastical and fictional—or as some saw it, untrue. I like to think of the first novels as the reality TV of their day. People might have turned to them as a guilty pleasure, but they wouldn't have necessarily admitted it, at least not in the best society. (How wonderful, then, that the Austen family embraced novels, and were "not ashamed" to do so. From the beginning, Jane was in an environment that allowed her gifts to flourish.)

As you can imagine with the birth of this new art form, there were growing pains. Many novels were ponderous and weighty with long sections unrelated to the story. (These thousand-page tomes were so long that they are now nearly unreadable to modern audiences.) When her own "light & bright & sparkling" *Pride and Prejudice* came out, Austen joked that perhaps it needed "to be stretched out here & there with a long Chapter . . . of solemn specious nonsense . . . an Essay on Writing, a critique on Walter Scott, or the history of Buonaparte . . ."[2] In addition, many protagonists in these new novels were impossibly contrived. Heroines especially were of such perfect character that they never made any mistakes; they were lily white and untouchable, and their adventures were incredibly unrealistic as well.

I have no doubt that Jane read them and knew in her heart that she could do better. What a strange and unbelievable thing, when you think about it, for a plain girl from the country with little education to think that she could tackle a relatively new art form and set it right. But that is just about what she did. She wrote her stories, and not only gave us the beautiful characters we love but also changed the course of literature. She focused on real people, in real living situations, with real faults. She made them compelling. She captured their quirky characters so that even today we recognize them. She kept them short (I hear English Lit students groaning, but yes, compared to Richardson, Austen's novels are short, so count your blessings), and "sparkling." She showed us what fiction could be.

All because she nurtured her dreams.

Follow your love.

Austen started writing at age eleven, sharply funny stories that show her humor and confidence. She wrote because she couldn't *not* write. It's hard for us to imagine the strictures that were placed on women in the eighteenth century. We no longer wear corsets—unless you count Spanx—and we have no idea the kind of suffocating pressure society placed on a woman. Not only are we now allowed to vote and to work, but we're allowed to be fully part of the world and to do things that some consider more masculine in nature—like joining the military or playing in a punk band. There's no longer any requirement that we be ladies, so to speak, just because we are women. Not so for Austen. She was expected to be a lady, and a lady would never have written fiction. For one thing, from a religious standpoint, fiction's value was questionable. But for another, it required far too great a knowledge of the world and of the frailties of human nature. No real lady should have had the knowledge necessary to write good fiction.

One of Jane's favorite writers, Fanny Burney, burned everything she had written at the age of fifteen—including her first novel—because she was ashamed of her bad habit. It was so vulgar for a lady to write that Burney's family urged her to quit. Burney continued writing, flouting the mores of the day. There was just something inside that had to come out, regardless.

Austen was very proper in other regards, but not so concerned about being proper that she ever considered giving up her writing. Societal pressures didn't stop Jane. Her love—her writing, her characters—needed to be expressed and take form. Their life in her imagination wasn't enough, they had to be shared with the world. Writing was a constant presence in Jane's life. At her core, foremost, she was a writer. Thank God she didn't ignore that great love.

Be brave.

It's far easier to see our goals as a far-off possibility than to actually accomplish them. Perhaps it would have been easier for Jane not to write, especially in light of the way society viewed women writers. But how bereft would we be without Austen's stories? What if she had never ventured to pick up her pen?

It takes a brave soul to move from dreaming to doing. I think part of what aided Austen's bravery is that initially she saw writing not as work—not as the thing that would establish her forever in the annals of English literature—but as fun. She wrote to entertain herself and to make her family laugh. She didn't have to worry about being successful, with all the pressure that brings, and she didn't really need to worry about anyone outside her family circle learning that she wrote.

Still, it would have been very simple for Jane to sit in her home in the country, reading novels and thinking that someday maybe she would try that, but never actually doing anything about it. Her whole life could have gone by—except that she was brave enough to do what she really wanted to do.

Lizzy Bennet in *Pride and Prejudice* captures Austen's spirit in many ways. I love the scene where Lady Catherine de Bourgh comes to the Bennet home to intimidate Elizabeth into never marrying Darcy. Elizabeth's response is full of strength: "I am not to be intimidated," she tells Lady Catherine. "I am only resolved to act in that manner, which will, in my own opinion, constitute my happiness, without any reference to *you,* or to any person so wholly unconnected with me."[3]

Austen was not to be intimidated as well. Her own happiness in writing drove her to be brave enough to do it, regardless of what anyone else thought.

Do the unexpected.

If Jane Austen had done only what was expected of her, she would have left behind only some nice needlework. She would have quilted, gardened, helped her brothers take care of their growing broods of children, and sewn clothes for those in her family who needed them. She would have played the piano—which she did, though not terribly well, it seems. She would have helped to run the household. She would not have written six novels.

Perhaps women are more beholden to the expectations of others than men are. We like to please people, we don't want our parents or husbands or children to be disappointed in us. We don't want to cause friction. So we carry around this weight, and sometimes we let those expectations serve as the guiding force in our lives, more than what we sense to be our calling, more than our own gifts and talents and desires. As women, not only are we good at ferreting out others' hopes for us, but sometimes we also simply assume what they are, without ever discussing them. It's possible that when you break from the expected—when you step out of your given role to pursue your gifts—it won't be the least bit unwelcome. After all, Austen's pursuit of her own talent certainly wasn't unwelcome, at least not to her family, who rejoiced in her writing.

Again, Austen gives this spirit of hers to many of her characters. Elizabeth Bennet, as Lady Catherine made clear, was not to marry Mr. Darcy. Anne Elliot, in *Persuasion,* had allowed herself once to be guided away from the man she loved, and wasn't going to allow that again. Lady Russell expects her to love Mr. Elliot, but Anne constantly questions him, and in the end turns out to be right in her assessment of his character. In *Mansfield Park,* Fanny Price is supposed to take the very eligible offer of marriage from Henry Crawford, but even the expectations of her wealthy, sometimes domineering uncle will not force her into a relationship she's not sure about. Austen makes it clear that the expectations of others are not necessarily the best guiding force for your life.

Treasure the people who believe in you.

Society at large didn't make it necessarily easy to do what Jane did, but she was fortunate to have a great amount of support at home.

Her dearest friend and biggest fan was her older sister, Cassandra. The only two girls in a family with six boys, they were close from the time they were very small. In fact, when the Austen parents decided to send Cassandra to a boarding school, they reluctantly sent Jane along as well, in spite of the fact that she was too young. As Mrs. Austen said, "If Cassandra's head had been going to be cut off, Jane would have her's [*sic*] cut off too."[4]

Cassandra would have always known what Jane was working on and would have been the first to read it. Cassandra actually made it possible for Jane to be a writer by assuming most of the responsibilities around the home, allowing Jane time to write. As their mother aged and the girls took over the household, Jane's only responsibilities were to handle breakfast and to manage the sugar, tea, and wine stores, which would have left Cassandra with considerably more work. We can presume that Jane didn't keep any secrets from Cassandra, even about the career that she tried to hide from the rest of the world.

Jane's father cheered her on from the very beginning. At least one of the notebooks in which Jane copied her early stories was a gift from her father, as was most likely the writing desk she used throughout her life, now on display at the British Library in London. Whether or not Jane would have been published without her father's encouragement is an interesting question. It was Mr. Austen who first proudly and expectantly sent off one of Jane's manuscripts (*First Impressions,* later to become *Pride and Prejudice*) to a publishing house in London.

In later years, Jane's brother Henry—a charming, good-looking, well-connected, man-about-town—took over all of her publishing negotiations and handled her professional affairs. Henry was so darn proud that he let slip that his very own sister was the author of the popular *Pride and Prejudice,* against Jane's specific wishes. The other brothers loved and encouraged her as well, and Mrs. Austen couldn't resist reading aloud from *Pride and Prejudice* to a neighbor immediately after its release. (Jane admired her enthusiasm but complained that she got the voices all wrong.)

There's no doubt that Jane Austen's books exist in large part because of the great support of her family. Jane loved them dearly, and was content to have them form the largest part of her social circle. Along with a few close friends, they were all Jane needed. The joy Jane's family took in her writing no doubt gave her satisfaction, along with the freedom and desire to write more.

Do what you would be willing to be poor for.

Perhaps this is the rub for our twenty-first-century selves. When Jane Austen started writing, she had no concept of making money at it. She wrote merely to entertain her family, with little thought of publishing. Surely as a twelve-year-old writing her *Juvenilia* stories that was the case.

Even when she first published at thirty-five, after many years of trying, she was required to pay for the publication of *Sense and Sensibility* herself. She didn't have to actually lay out any money, but had the book failed, she would have been expected to make up the difference. She saved from her meager income to have enough of a cushion in case the book didn't sell at all. Of the four novels published during Jane's lifetime, three of them were essentially self-published or published on commission. Only *Pride and Prejudice* was purchased outright by the publisher. (And Jane would have made more money on that one had she self-published it.)

In her entire writing career, Jane Austen made roughly £670. As a young woman, she was used to receiving an annual allowance of £20 from her father, so the amount she made wasn't insignificant, but neither was it life changing. She liked to joke and say things like, "I have now therefore written myself into £250.—which only makes me long for more."[5] I don't think she would have complained about making more money, but I also don't think she thought about it all that much. Her dream was simply to write. If she made money at it, so much the better.

In contrast, we seem to immediately associate our dreams with fame and fortune. In fact, we may mistake being famous and rich as being the ultimate dream. (Shame on us! Austen would love the ridiculousness that can lead to.) We assume that whatever brings us acclaim and lots of money will make us happy. But stop and consider: Are you doing something you would be willing to be poor for?

That's a powerful thing, to break away from thoughts of money and do something simply because it fulfills you, because it's what you were meant to do. If money were no object, if money didn't exist, what would you do?

It's important to love what you do for its own sake, rather than to love it because it makes you rich. Certainly that was the case with Austen. She made little money at it, but she kept writing because money—as nice as it would have been—wasn't really the point.

Persist.

Because we have hindsight, and we know what a huge literary star Jane Austen became, it's tempting to sort of read her story backwards and assume that all of her literary life was a huge success. After all, if she truly is one of the greatest English writers (and she is), she wouldn't have had any trouble getting published, right?

Oh, so wrong. Austen's road to publication was full of travail. Without the encouragement of her family, she might have given up.

When a twenty-one-year-old Austen finished her second novel, *First Impressions,* she read it to her family in the evenings. They loved it. Her father loved it so much, he must have thought it was just as good as—better, even, than—other published novels, so he sent a letter describing it to a publisher in London. He asked what it would cost to publish it "at the Author's risk," or if the publisher might be willing to buy it. Said letter came back quickly to the Austen home with a note across the top, "declined by Return of Post."[6] Austen's first foray into publishing was met with impersonal rejection.

Six years later, when Jane had finished her third book, *Susan* (later to become *Northanger Abbey*), her family cajoled and encouraged until she was once again willing to try for publication. Crosby & Co. in London gave her ten pounds (a pittance for a novel, even if it did amount to half of Jane's annual allowance) for the manuscript and promised "early publication."[7] Jane's brother Henry assisted with this deal and in all of her publishing negotiations from this point on, and I wonder if the *Northanger Abbey* manuscript might have been chosen because Henry Tilney—the witty, sharp hero of the novel—resembled Jane's brother Henry himself.

At any rate, the promised "early publication" was a farce. Crosby & Co. advertised Jane's novel but never published it. So Jane waited and waited, no doubt anxious and eager to see her first book in print.

She waited six full years, and still nothing. Unable to take it anymore, she sent a letter inquiring about her book and asking if the publisher needed another copy of the manuscript. Because the publisher did not know her name, she could sign the letter with any name she wanted. She chose Mrs. Ashton Dennis, and signed only with her initials—MAD. Crosby & Co. sent a horrible letter back, saying, "There was not any time stipulated for its publication, neither are we bound to publish it."[8] They offered to sell it back to her for the ten pounds they originally paid for it and told her that if she attempted to publish it elsewhere without first buying back the rights, they would "take proceedings to stop the sale." After six years of waiting, now thirty-three years old, this kind of answer must have been more than disheartening.[9]

We don't have a record of how Jane's first successful publishing contract came to be, but we know that sometime in the winter of 1810–11, Jane received a contract for the very first novel she had written: *Sense and Sensibility.* There were still more inexplicable delays—this time in months, rather than years. Originally scheduled for release in May 1811, the book didn't actually come out until the very end of October. At that point Jane was thirty-five and had been writing for nearly twenty-five years.

So yes, Jane Austen, one of the greatest writers in the English language, had a hard time getting published. It would have been very easy for her to give up, to just write her stories and read them to her family, to avoid the publishing world that had been harsh and cruel. She didn't do that. She persisted.

Temper your expectations.

Another error we modern women tend to make—maybe this is strictly an American thing—is that when we begin to dream we have a tendency to assume that we will be wildly successful. We write a book thinking it will be a best seller. We move to Hollywood to become a star. We begin a company confident that we will sell it two years later for millions. We become lawyers and expect to someday sit on the Supreme Court. Jane would no doubt tell us to temper our expectations.

Marianne Dashwood in *Sense and Sensibility* with her romantic state of mind would understand entirely. You know, it's possible to be romantic about things other than romance—to get carried away by wishes until they become expectations. This is precisely the way Marianne and her mother behaved. Jane tells us, "What Marianne and her mother conjectured one moment, they believed the next—that with them, to wish was to hope, and to hope was to expect."[10]

Don't you think we do that, too? Our wishes become hopes, which immediately become expectations. Our imaginations "outstrip . . . the truth"[11] as Jane would say. Of course, all of Marianne's unrealistic expectations center on marriage, but we have to consider the fact that those were the only expectations Marianne was allowed to have in that day and age. She had no hope of a career. She loved music and loved to play the piano, but would never have considered performing for money. I have no doubt that if Austen were writing today, she would find a lot of humor in the other ways we deceive ourselves and play the fool in our fame-and-fortune dreams.

Jane would urge us—in our relationships and in our pursuits—not to be foolish. The word *foolish* may not be in vogue any longer, but it was a concept that would have been very alive and well to Jane. Many of the arcs of her characters' stories revolve around their own foolishness and the trouble it gets them into. Most of our dreams will require years of hard work that will often go unrewarded. Of course there are exceptions, but we would be wiser not to expect those. As an Austen girl your first goal should be to be wise.

Those who begin pursuing their dreams with ridiculously high expectations will likely not have the endurance to finish the course. Jane saw very little of her own fame during her lifetime. Had her expectations been too high—had she had her heart set on being known forever as one of the greatest English writers—she would no doubt have become discouraged and given up. Jane didn't allow her heart to get carried away. She was prudent and wise. She worked hard and was grateful for every success, however small.

Share your gifts with the world.

So this sounds a bit daunting, no? When you follow your dream you will likely work very hard for very little money. You will face rejection—probably multiple times. Your talents and skills may never be recognized. Even within your own family, people may think you're crazy. Like Jane, you may have cause to get MAD.

Yet, our blessed Jane has one final challenge for you when it comes to those dreams of yours: Share your gifts with the world. Had Jane not braved the publishing world that had proven to be so uncaring, her stories might have wound up as moldy manuscripts in the attic. They may have been passed down from one generation of Austens to the next, remembered only as the stories of their dear Aunt Jane. How much would the world have lost then?

Austen loved being published and the small amount of fame her books received. She joked about Walter Scott, beloved and best-selling writer: "Walter Scott has no business to write novels, especially good ones.—It is not fair.—He has Fame & Profit enough as a Poet, and should not be taking the bread out of other people's mouths.—I do not like him . . ."[12] But however much she liked to laugh about a little friendly rivalry with one of the best writers of the day and complain about her paltry income, her great joy was in the writing itself. When *Pride and Prejudice* was published, she called it "my own darling Child,"[13] and of *Sense and Sensibility,* she wrote, "I can no more forget it, than a mother can forget her suckling child."[14] Jane's precious books—her darling children—gave her great satisfaction.

It must be said that as an eighteenth-century girl Jane had one advantage over us: She had no need to work. As a woman in that era, she would never have been allowed to work, but that restriction meant that in whatever time she had to herself (and she had more of it because of her sister Cassandra's help), she was free to write. We, on the other hand, hold down jobs that take increasingly more time to foot the bill for our apartments, cars, and groceries. We make our own meals—something Jane would rarely have had to do—and wash our own clothes and are entirely self-sufficient, which leaves us somewhat less time both for dreaming and for doing. It's strange to think that, in that way at least, the eighteenth century actually had one advantage for women.

Jane's other stroke of luck was that what she wanted to do—write stories—had only in the last fifty years become actually possible, or even thought of. And even though she wasn't supposed to write since she was a woman, at least she could write in secret, in the privacy of her home. If Jane had yearned to be an accountant, that simply could never have happened. Our great advantage, of course, is that there's very little we can't do today. We have none of those eighteenth-century restrictions about what is proper for a lady and what isn't. We have access to every realm of life. We are free to dream and do just about anything we want.

Jane would tell us above all things to be sensible, wise, humble, and brave—and to follow our hearts.

CHAPTER 2

Becoming a Woman of Substance

Jane Austen was not the prettiest or the wealthiest woman. Her clothes would not have been the latest fashion, and her drawing and singing (if she did any at all) were not up to society's standards for the truly accomplished lady. She didn't have a fat inheritance with which to attract a suitor. But these shortcomings didn't faze her. She was not interested in being one of those women for whom a fine dress and a silly, rich husband would suffice. What she wanted to be—what she was—was a woman of substance.

First and foremost, Austen was sensible. She didn't feed her romantic imagination to excess. She thought for herself and could manage an intelligent conversation in spite of never having had a serious education. She was hardly perfect—her exquisite wit could also be cruel—but she was guided through the various trials of eighteenth-century life by an inner character that was always striving for improvement. Her Christian faith helped to form her and gave her the hope of grace, helping her understand that faults could be forgiven and changed. In a world in which the ephemera of wealth and status could consume one's life, Austen was concerned with being substantive: thoughtful, honest, kind, wise.

It's tempting to think that our world is so different from the staid and proper eighteenth century that Jane called home. We value people for how much money they make, how beautiful they are, and how famous they become. If they're famous, they can get away with just about anything. For many people, life goals can be summed up as achieving celebrity and making a lot of money. If it takes a little bending of the rules to reach those goals, a fair share of people are willing to do that. And people barely expect their politicians to be honest anymore. The importance of *character* as a concept in our national conversation is somewhat questionable.

But actually, that could almost describe Jane's eighteenth-century world as well. People were valued almost exclusively based on how much they were worth. A common life goal was simply to become rich—whether that meant marrying for money (not love), or ingratiating themselves with people who had money. Those who had money, along with a place in society, could get away with cruelty. Without Twitter, YouTube, and reality TV, fame on a grand scale was not so easy to achieve in the eighteenth century, but it's apparent that the best character traits—kindness, humility, modesty—were still not as abundant as we might imagine, given that century's emphasis on them. We may not be so far removed from Austen's world as we imagine.

This desire for a substantive life forms the backbone for Austen's novels as well. Like Austen herself, her heroines were not the wealthiest or the prettiest, and they may have been saddled with some rather unfortunate relatives—a la *Pride and Prejudice*'s bumbling and ridiculous Mr. Collins. But you can count on an Austen heroine to be sensible, or at least to learn to be sensible throughout the course of the novel.

Her leading ladies actually make something of themselves, in spite of their often drab and occasionally dire predicaments. In spite of great odds against them, each heroine marries well and marries for love—of course, in Austen's time, the only way a woman could make something of herself was to marry well. But there's another subtler success story woven into the background of each Austen novel: that of a woman coming to know herself, being willing to admit some occasionally great failings, and setting them right.

Not only do Austen's characters find love, they find themselves, and they improve themselves. They see their faults in ways they haven't before. They realize what kinds of things they are capable of—and that at times they are capable of doing things badly—and this awareness spurs them to change. It's a testament to Austen's greatness as a writer that none of her stories read like morality tales; they're never moralistic or tedious (except perhaps *Mansfield Park,* in my humble opinion). But when you look closely, the heart and soul of each novel is about the heroine's (and the hero's) character—about her substance, her worth. Through these stories, Austen's voice echoes down to us today.

Don't be silly.

One thing Austen had little patience for was silliness. Laughter and wit are supreme in Austen's world, but silliness is something different. It represents that brand of woman with nary a thought in her head, who fails to think at all seriously about life. In regards to spending time with Miss Eliza Moore, Austen wrote, "We shall not have two Ideas in common. She is young, pretty, chattering, & thinking cheifly [*sic*] (I presume) of Dress, Company, & Admiration."[15] Austen wanted her friends to be capable of thinking about bigger things.

Austen's commentary on this can be seen in *Pride and Prejudice*'s chattering Lydia Bennet, the poster child for everything silly and foolish. Perhaps Lydia didn't have much of a chance. Austen describes her as "a stout, well-grown girl of fifteen, with a fine complexion and good-humoured countenance"[16]—and of all five Bennet sisters, Lydia is the tallest. But that's where the blessings of Lydia's birth end. If she was good-looking, she was also born with a strong will, an indolent spirit, and a determination to never listen and never learn. Her mother—not exactly a paragon of sense herself—saw nothing wrong with Lydia and mistook her foolhardiness for simple good-naturedness. Her father, although he clearly saw Lydia's faults, was too lazy himself to bother to correct them. So where her mother encouraged and her father ignored, Lydia was free to fully explore every foolishness she stumbled into. No one could have imagined that this impulsiveness would eventually lead her into the arms and bed of Mr. Wickham.

For quite a while, Lydia had been falling in love with whichever officer in the militia happened to be paying her the most attention at the time. In Brighton that leading role belonged to Wickham, and when he proposed that they elope, Lydia eagerly jumped at the chance. Of course, Wickham had no intention of marrying Lydia, but he'd incurred enough gambling debts that it was convenient for him to make an escape. And if he could have company along the way, even if it ruined a foolish girl's reputation, so much the better. So Lydia—"Vain, ignorant, idle, and absolutely uncontrolled!"[17]—runs off, with no thought to her own reputation and no understanding that she didn't have enough money to tempt Wickham into marriage. Silly, silly girl. Had Darcy not intervened and bribed Wickham to follow through with a wedding, Lydia would have been ruined forever, destined to a shameful existence with no hope of any husband.

Lydia remains foolish to the end, oblivious to the debt she owes to everyone who has rescued her, ungrateful and sure that her sisters envy her because of her handsome husband, putting on airs as the youngest and first married of them all. But Austen tells us, "with such an husband, her misery was considered certain."[18] Their affection soon vanished, they never lived within their means, and Lydia was in the habit of boldly writing to ask her better-off sisters for money. Whether or not Lydia ever contemplated the consequences of her actions, whether she thought about the fact that her life could have turned out differently, is uncertain, but to the reader it's clear that her foolish, youthful misstep has ruined any chance of real happiness.

Here in the twenty-first century we have some advantages over Lydia, especially in the way that youthful indiscretions—infatuations with our own Mr. Wickhams—can remain just that; we don't need to fear that one wrong step will bind us for life and doom us to marital misery. But foolish impulses still have repercussions, and there are still men out there who gladly use women and toss them aside. Austen's lesson here is that the more aware we are of our own potential for foolishness, the more we tame those impulses, the better our chances of happiness.

Value people for their character, regardless of how society labels them.

Popularity contests in the eighteenth century were rather cut and dry: If you had money and rank, you were destined to be sought after. Austen knew that the value of a person couldn't be quite so quickly or neatly assayed. She was determined to see beyond society's labels to a person's true worth.

Austen was in a unique position similar to that of Elizabeth Bennet in *Pride and Prejudice:* Her father was a gentleman, but not at all wealthy. Actually, the Bennets were much better off than the Austens were. Jane's family never slipped into poverty, but they were never really secure, either. The Austen home was very simple, but Jane also spent time with her brother Edward and his family, where she was surrounded by everything rich. (Edward had been adopted by wealthy relatives who couldn't have children of their own, so he inherited their estates.) From this vantage point, Jane got to know people both at the bottom and the top of the social ladder.

As she gained friends low and high, she came to respect and love them—despite their poverty and never solely because of their wealth. She loved Mrs. Knight, her brother Edward's wealthy adopted mother, along with other members of that rich branch of the family. Another dear friend, Anne Sharp, was a governess who used to tend Edward's children. Although Anne didn't work for Edward's family long, she and Jane kept in touch for the rest of Jane's life. In one of Jane's last surviving letters, she writes to her as "my dearest Anne"[19]—a sign of their close friendship. When Jane died, Anne was one of few who received a lock of her hair.

Fleshing out her ideas on how to correctly value people, Austen gives us a tale of two characters in *Persuasion:* a Mrs. Smith of Westgate Buildings and Viscountess Lady Dalrymple of Laura Place. Mrs. Smith is no one, a widow with no distinguished surname who lost everything when her husband, who had driven them into poverty, died. She has encountered setback after setback and is in Bath to see if the healing waters will help her rheumatism, which has temporarily paralyzed her. She lives in one room in a boardinghouse, is unable to move without help, and has no friends. (In writing about Mrs. Smith's ill health, Austen may even have thought of her friend Anne Sharp, who struggled for years and had to leave several jobs due to poor health.)

But Mrs. Smith, as low as she is, has a claim on our heroine Anne Elliot: When Anne came to school in Bath at the age of fourteen, homesick and grieving her mother's recent death, Mrs. Smith, then unmarried, took her under her wing and gave her comfort during that dark time.

High at the other end of Bath's social scene, Lady Dalrymple lives in fashionable Laura Place. She is also a widow, but that is where the similarity ends. As a viscountess, Lady Dalrymple's worth is earned for her by her title. She is guaranteed an elevated place in society. Everyone who can will seek her acquaintance and treasure it. Regardless of what she is like, Lady Dalrymple will be adored. Which is a good thing for her—Austen implies that without her title and its guaranteed social standing, Lady Dalrymple would have little hope.

Leave it to Austen to turn the social structure on its head. The woman everyone is expected to revere is vacuous and dull, while the poor cripple who spends her days in the tiny room of a boardinghouse ought to be treasured. Many if not most people in Anne's position would have evaluated the situation based on what they stood to gain. Acquaintance with the Viscountess Lady Dalrymple would by association give Anne a higher place in society, allow her to meet other high-ranking people and generally move up the social ladder. But Anne has Austen's heart: She sees little value in the viscountess and actually snubs her in favor of her old, sick friend—hardly self-seeking.

In one of Austen's ironic twists, Anne's friendship with Mrs. Smith is essential to the happy resolution of the novel. Only Mrs. Smith can reveal to Anne the true character of the man everyone wants her to marry—William Elliot, heir to her father's title and another person whom society has completely misjudged. Mr. Elliot has money and respectability; on the outside he appears to be all graciousness and gentlemanly behavior. Only Mrs. Smith—who knew Mr. Elliot through her husband for more than a decade—can confirm Anne's suspicions about his true nature. She describes him as "a man without heart or conscience; a designing, wary, cold-blooded being, who thinks only of himself."[20] Mr. Elliot had helped to lead her husband into all kinds of extravagances, and then had disappeared as soon as their money did.

With Mrs. Smith's insight, there is no chance that she could ever be persuaded into becoming his wife. Poor, sickly Mrs. Smith gives Anne the valuable truth that validates Anne's decision, that helps protect her from marrying the wrong man and from the life of misery that would have followed. Had Anne valued the viscountess more than her old friend, there's no telling how the story may have ended—but Anne, being Anne, would never have done that. Like Austen, she put social standing—popularity—aside and valued people first by their character.

WHEN THE RIGHT THING HURTS, DO IT ANYWAY.

At this point, Austen with all of her lofty principles may be starting to sound a bit like your mother. Don't hold it against her. One of the measuring sticks Austen uses for sizing up someone's character is looking at how she behaves when the right thing, the thing she should do, is not in her best interest. It's what Austen expected of herself and what she gave to the best of her characters. Two of her leading lights in that regard are Elinor Dashwood and Edward Ferrars in *Sense and Sensibility.* The fact that they both pass this test with more than flying colors and then wind up together is poignantly sweet.

Elinor and Edward, of course, meet at Norland Park after Elinor's father dies. Edward has come to visit his sister Fanny, whose husband John (Elinor's half-brother) has just inherited the estate. When Edward and Elinor begin spending more time together, clearly falling in love, Fanny steps in to separate them. She drops some rude, very clear hints about what kind of woman Edward is expected to marry (i.e., someone with much more money and social standing than Elinor). Mrs. Dashwood and her daughters quickly leave. They still expect Edward to visit them at their new home in Devonshire and are left to wonder why he delays his visit, and why he is reserved, cold, and unhappy when he finally comes.

Why would Edward develop such a close friendship-bordering-romance with Elinor and then avoid her? The answer to that riddle lies with the flirty and frivolous Lucy Steele, who corners Elinor on a walk at Barton Park and, under the guise of friendship, unburdens herself to her. For four years, Lucy and Edward have been engaged, since they met at her uncle's house in Plymouth when Edward was in school there. Sly Lucy can have no doubt as to what is really going on. She must understand Elinor's attachment to Edward. (Sir John Middleton has nearly disclosed the whole thing, in the name of mirth.) With her supposedly friendly confession, she is staking a claim, making it clear that however little contact she's had with Edward lately, and however better suited Elinor may be to the match, Elinor's hopes must be dashed. As one final painful stroke, she requires that Elinor keep the engagement a secret, and tell no one.

Elinor feels herself bound by her promise to Lucy, with a compunction that forbids her to tell anyone at all—even those closest to her, her mother and sister, who continue to speculate about Edward and his feelings for her. However capable Elinor is at managing her emotions with her "unceasing exertion,"[21] Lucy inflicted months of pain.

If there are degrees of painful promises, Edward's is worse. Elinor knows, "if her case were pitiable, his was hopeless."[22] He made the engagement to Lucy when he was young and susceptible and a bit foolish. Now he knows that he is not in love with her, now he knows that he could have been truly happy with someone so much better than Lucy Steele—with Elinor—but he won't allow himself to go back on his word.

I have to say, to me both of these seem like foolish promises to keep. It seems like Elinor could have fudged a little and told her mother and sister Marianne what was going on, so they could understand and help tend her broken heart. And it seems terrible that Edward would be willing to marry Lucy, whom he acknowledges he no longer loves. What good could come from that, except a miserable life with a silly, manipulating wife? Wouldn't Lucy herself be better off if she married someone who actually loved her? But in the eighteenth century, one's word was a bond, and both Edward and Elinor are determined that whatever the cost to them, their word will not be meaningless.

Of course, everything works out in the end. When Edward's mother discovers his secret engagement, she disinherits him. Lucy Steele's affections follow the money and instantly land on Edward's younger brother Robert, who will now inherit the estate that would have gone to Edward. (Unlike Elinor and Edward, Lucy is determined to do only what is in her own best interest.) Lucy marries Robert, leaving Edward and Elinor poor but very happy that they can now have the only thing they ever really wanted—to be together. More than that, they have the comfort of being absolutely certain of the other's character. Austen tells us, "Elinor gloried in his integrity."[23] No doubt Austen herself did as well.

Be a good conversationalist.

As Anne Elliot reminds us in *Persuasion,* "good company . . . is the company of clever, well-informed people, who have a great deal of conversation . . ." One can't imagine Jane Austen being anything other than the best conversationalist. Though she was shy with strangers, once let into her world one would have met with large doses of humor and lively discussion from a compassionate and caring friend. She wrote jokingly to her sister, "Expect a most agreable [*sic*] Letter; for not being overburdened with subject—(having nothing at all to say)—I shall have no check to my Genius from beginning to end."[24] But her letters actually are genius, full of wit and whimsy about the daily details—the struggles and joys—of life. Reading them, one is left in no doubt that Austen's conversation would have been full of energy and charm. And while she also joked that it was her "unhappy fate seldom to treat people so well as they deserve,"[25] she doles out tenderness and empathy along with that cheerful banter.

Through the words she puts in her characters' mouths, Austen teaches us both what good conversation is and what it is not. Lydia Bennet, for example, is a horrible conversationalist because she refuses to listen to anyone and talks only about herself. Lydia is "a most determined talker,"[26] but *talking* and *conversing* are two entirely different things. Conversing requires the ability to listen, to demonstrate genuine concern for the other person. But Lydia of course is a complete failure at that: "She seldom listened to anybody for more than half a minute."[27] Likewise, Mary Elliot in *Persuasion* can think only of herself, how sick she imagines herself to be, and how she is being wronged by other people. She only sees the negative. A conversation with Mary always includes reassuring her that no one has slighted her, that she has no reason to be angry. Mary always needs to be talked down from something. As a result, no one really wants to talk to her. Witty Elizabeth Bennet is perhaps Austen's best conversationalist (and perhaps most like Austen in that regard), with her sharp sense of humor and quick tongue. Even she would admit, however, that her use of that skill is occasionally misdirected, as she derided Darcy and praised Wickham, and initially got everything wrong.

Austen also gives us examples of those who communicate well. In *Sense and Sensibility,* Marianne learns from Elinor's example to extend kindness (or at least civility) in the midst of her own pain, even to those who may not entirely deserve it. *Persuasion*'s Anne Elliot is another who sets aside her own broken heart to be part of the conversations around her. That's not to imply that her world is all pain and self-sacrifice: Anne finds genuine friendship and joy in her relationships with the Musgrove family and Admiral and Mrs. Croft.

Austen teaches us that conversation is essentially kindness put into words. It requires listening and compassion, requires that we step out of ourselves for a moment and pull our attention away from our own pain or joy in order to partake in the lives of those around us. In our own more open world, we'll have more to talk about and less to hide, because we can share just about everything, at least with our closest friends. (We generally have no need to hide a secret engagement or conceal a broken heart the way Austen's characters did.) But the basic rules of conversational kindness will always be the same.

Know yourself.

Perhaps Austen's best advice for us would be summed up in these two words: *Know yourself.* And by that, she wouldn't intend for us to delve into the deep emotional self-knowledge we cultivate today. (We're better in our century at understanding what comprises our emotional struggles and sorting out those kinds of inner tangles.) Instead, Austen would be referring to a moral self-awareness that for her was motivated in large part by her Christian faith. She was driven by an intense desire to understand her own failings and by God's grace to correct them. This desire is nowhere more clear than in one of the evening prayers she penned. In the language of her Christian faith, echoing the Anglican prayerbook she knew so well, Austen writes:

Teach us to understand the sinfulness of our own hearts, and bring to our knowledge every fault of temper and every evil habit in which we have indulged to the discomfort of our fellow-creatures . . . May we now, and on each return of night, consider how the past day has been spent by us, what have been our prevailing thoughts, words and actions during it, and how far we can acquit ourselves of evil. . . . have we neglected any known duty, or willingly given pain to any human being? Incline us to ask our hearts these questions oh! God, and save us from deceiving ourselves by pride or vanity.[28]

This trait binds her heroines; this willingness—even eagerness—to search their souls, to understand their motives, to strive to live up to their own high standards and to understand their weak spots. And because this is Austen, of course, sometimes those weaknesses can only be pointed out by the men who would be their husbands.

Emma Woodhouse shares what I think may have been Austen's own weakness. Lively Emma lacked nothing in terms of conversational power, but she occasionally abused that power, as when she attacked poor Miss Bates for her own effusive talkativeness. As Austen scholar R.W. Chapman notes, "Miss Austen can be exquisitely wicked."[29] In one letter, Jane writes of Mrs. Hall who had a stillborn child. She says it was "oweing to a fright.—I suppose she happened unawares to look at her husband."[30] Austen gives some of that sharp edge to Emma.

Emma and her friends may have had "a very fine day"[31] for their picnic at Box Hill, but they wouldn't have any harmony in their party. Mr. and Mrs. Elton bristled at everything Emma said. Frank Churchill was resenting his secret engagement to Jane Fairfax, and Jane was silently devastated. Emma herself was thoughtless and bored. Frank flirts with Emma to ignite Jane's ire and tells everyone in Emma's name that they must come up with "one thing very clever . . . or two things moderately clever—or three things very dull indeed." To which voluble Miss Bates replies, "Oh! very well, then I need not be uneasy. . . . I shall be sure to say three dull things as soon as ever I open my mouth, shan't I?" Austen tells us, "Emma could not resist. 'Ah! ma'am, but there may be a difficulty. Pardon me—but you will be limited as to number—only three at once.'" Miss Bates eventually catches her meaning, and blushes, afraid to find that she "must make [herself] very disagreeable" and determined to "try to hold [her] tongue."[32]

Emma is used to being coddled and flattered, but Mr. Knightley, who observed the whole exchange, will have none of it. As they walk back to their carriages, Mr. Knightley admonishes her. "I cannot see you acting wrong, without a remonstrance," he says. "How could you be so unfeeling to Miss Bates? How could you be so insolent . . .? It was badly done, indeed! . . . to have you now, in thoughtless spirits, and the pride of the moment, laugh at her, humble her . . . I will tell you truths while I can." Emma is "most forcibly struck." Austen tells us, "Never had she felt so agitated, mortified, grieved . . . The truth of his representation there was no denying. She felt it at her heart."[33] Emma rides home in uncharacteristic tears, learning from Mr. Knightley's rebuke not only how wrong she had been that day, but how wrong her thoughts had been for so long—knowing herself more clearly. She might have stated with Elizabeth Bennet, after she realizes her own pride and the errors it has led to, "Till this moment, I never knew myself."[34]

Austen may have needed a rebuke like Mr. Knightley's herself, may have even received one at some point. She wanted herself and her characters to be aware of their "every evil habit," to know themselves clearly. She would want that for us as well.

Give yourself grace and be happy.

If Austen is anxious that we recognize our own faults, she doesn't want us to brood on them unnecessarily. Again, this comes in large part from Austen's Christian faith, which emphasized grace and forgiveness. In another of her evening prayers, Jane writes of a "Heavenly Father" who will be merciful, who understands "the infirmity of our nature, and the temptations which surround us."[35] Austen, who can admit that even dastardly Willoughby has a chance at being reasonably happy—with his wealthy wife and his hunting—wouldn't condemn her dear heroines to misery for their faults.

My favorite example of Austen's wish that we forgive ourselves can be seen in little Catherine Morland in *Northanger Abbey*.

With a head full of gothic romances and all their horror, Catherine goes to visit the Tilneys at old Northanger Abbey hoping and even "craving to be frightened."[36] She hears the story of their mother, who died far too early, presumably when all the children were gone, and sees that their father could have been cruel. With those bare facts, she fills in the rest of the story and doesn't hesitate to paint with a broad brush: The father tortured, even killed, his lovely wife, she concludes. So she goes to hunt for clues in the dead wife's room, and is startled in the midst of her search by the young Henry Tilney, who has returned home a day early.

Catherine Morland may have her faults, but being dishonest is not one of them. Unable to stand up to Henry's questioning, she confesses the whole thing—her suspicions of his father, her assumptions about his mother's untimely demise. Henry is horrified and sets her straight. Both he and his brother Frederick were home when his mother died. She had the best care possible. Yes, she was loved by his father, though perhaps differently and less tenderly than she may have wished.

Catherine is immediately ashamed of the story her imagination invented. But after this brief period with its "tears of shame,"[37] Catherine learns to hope. She doesn't forget the past, but determines never to repeat her foolish mistake. She begins to see that people's characters usually consist of "a general though unequal mixture of good and bad,"[38]—that, though the elder Mr. Tilney may not have been perfectly loving, that did not mean his heart harbored murderous tendencies.

Sweet Catherine, once she makes up her mind, has "nothing to do but to forgive herself and be happier than ever."[39] Austen, I'm sure, would recommend the same course for us: Recognize our faults, consider them, determine to change, and give ourselves the grace to be "happier than ever." She wouldn't have us mope or allow our failures to bury us in guilt. No—in Austen's world once we recognize a failure, we're meant to move beyond it. And for Austen, recognizing failure gives us that much more of a chance of actually being happy, from the improvement of our own character if nothing else.

Be prepared to laugh at yourself (and let others laugh with you).

If all this talk of being a woman of substance has you feeling that Austen is terribly serious, you can breathe easier—Austen would never be too serious to laugh. Laughter is an essential part of Austen's ethos, and if we're to live up to what she would want us to be, we have to be prepared not only to laugh at ourselves, but to let others join in the fun. She writes in one of her letters, "Whenever I fall into misfortune, how many jokes it ought to furnish to my acquaintance in general, or I shall die dreadfully in their debt for entertainment."[40] Mr. Bennet echoes her in *Pride and Prejudice:* "For what do we live, but to make sport for our neighbors and laugh at them in our turn?"[41]

Whatever our faults and failings, whatever scrapes or difficult situations we get ourselves into, however serious we may be about making sure our character is sound and our actions right, Austen would never want us to lose our sense of humor—or to deprive others of theirs. A woman of substance would never be too serious to laugh, especially at herself.

Chapter 3

Thinking about Love

Ah, love—that subject on which above all others we hope for Jane's help. The lively young Jane Austen was not without admirers, but actual love stories from her life are sparse and lacking in details. Many have heard of her flirtation with Tom Lefroy (dramatized in the movie *Becoming Jane*), but it may have been just that—a flirtation—rather than a great love that she carried with her and mourned for the rest of her life.

What we know of the story is this: Tom Lefroy was an Irishman who had just finished his degree in Dublin and was planning to study law. He came to Hampshire to stay with his uncle and aunt for the Christmas holidays when Jane had just turned twenty. Anne Lefroy, Tom's aunt by marriage, was Jane's dear friend and mentor; since the families were very close, a visitor and relative of the Lefroys would certainly have been introduced to the Austens and made to feel welcome there.

In Jane's words, Tom was "a very gentlemanlike, good-looking, pleasant young man."[42] I hate to disappoint those who loved the movie, but by all accounts Tom was actually a good guy, not the rake he's portrayed as being. Jane and Tom danced at three balls over the course of several weeks. Jane writes laughingly, "Imagine to yourself everything most profligate and shocking in the way of dancing and sitting down together."[43] If they showed each other undue attention, this is as "profligate" as things became. Tom was teased quite a bit about Jane at the Lefroy house, so that at times he attempted to avoid her. Jane did plenty of teasing herself, joking that Tom's "*one* fault" was "that his morning coat is a great deal too light"[44] and saying he wore it because he was such an admirer of Tom Jones and therefore wore the same color the fictional character wore.

Tom came from a large family of eleven children and was expected to do well, to help secure the future of the rest of his family. At twenty years old, Tom had yet to earn any money, and Jane had nothing, so the match could never go anywhere. When Anne Lefroy sensed the two were becoming attached, she stepped in and sent Tom to London. Family lore says that she was annoyed with him for leading on her friend when he knew he could never carry through with a match.

As Tom was about to leave, Jane wrote to Cassandra, "I rather expect to receive an offer from my friend in the course of the evening. I shall refuse him, however, unless he promises to give away his white Coat." And later, "At length the Day is come on which I am to flirt my last with Tom Lefroy, & when you receive this it will be over—My tears flow as I write, at the melancholy idea."[45] As always, Jane injects her heartbreak (faux or real—who can tell?) with the light lilt of humor. Her heart had been touched, but not so much that she couldn't laugh. Even the expected offer is likely just a joke. Jane liked Tom, certainly. Did she love him? That seems questionable. She saw him several times, danced with him, and flirted. It could have turned into something more serious, but it didn't. There are no further surviving letters mourning his loss, no record of a broken heart. As Jane's niece Caroline points out in a letter after Jane's death, Tom could have pursued Jane several years later when he had earned his fortune, if he had wanted to. He didn't, though, and it's unlikely Jane ever saw Tom again.

I think the great gift of Tom Lefroy in Austen's life was that he sparked her imagination. This flirtation gave her insight into the possibilities of love. What if a poor country girl wanted to marry someone who had no money? What if she fell in love with someone with an awful lot of money, whose family didn't approve? What kind of expectations should a girl in Austen's situation have, and could her character, her wit, be enough to win someone over? Austen may not have had the full experience of love, but she could imagine it, and the questions brought to her mind by this and other experiences fueled her writing. Ten months after Tom left for London, Jane started writing *Pride and Prejudice*—a story that must have been bubbling along in her mind.

Austen lived her life on the perimeter of romance—if at times it was a possibility, it never blossomed. But she became a student of love, and passes her lessons down to us in her books and letters. Some of them may surprise us.

Bring your sense of humor.

Love can be treacherous, it can be fretful, but it should be fun. Austen's letters about Tom Lefroy, brief as they are, are brimming with laughter. Granted, they're the letters of a twenty-year-old who has a few admirers and may just be beginning to feel her own romantic potential. At twenty, sorting through who liked her and who didn't, dancing with the guys she enjoyed, and trying desperately to avoid others, Austen had a lot to laugh about.

Jane writes to Cassandra, listing her partners after a ball, "To my inexpressible astonishment, I entirely escaped John Lyford. I was forced to fight hard for it, however." Always looking for humor in everyday things, she writes that her brother James "cut up the turkey last night with great perseverance."[46] Then, with mock magnanimity, she gives all her beaux save Tom Lefroy over to her friend Mary Lloyd:

> *Tell Mary that I make over Mr. Heartley & all his Estate to her for her sole use and Benefit in future, & not only him, but all my other Admirers into the bargain wherever she can find them, even the kiss which C. Powlett wanted to give me, as I mean to confine myself in future to Mr Tom Lefroy, for whom I do not care sixpence.*[47]

They aren't the letters of a girl who did a lot of pining; Austen chose to laugh instead. She would no doubt advise us not to take things quite so seriously, to spend less time yearning and more time enjoying the abundant humor of love.

QUESTION THE NATURE OF LOVE AT FIRST SIGHT.

Compared to Austen, we are a generation of hopeless romantics, just waiting to catch sight of the right person and fall head over heels into lifelong happiness. We may be surprised—Austen wouldn't have any of that. Actually, she doesn't give us any successful stories of love at first sight. Elizabeth Bennet in *Pride and Prejudice* gives "somewhat of a trial to [this] method, in her partiality for Wickham," but meets only with "ill-success."[48] She is charmed by his good looks and his red coat, and the fact that he has been ill-treated by Darcy makes her like him that much more. Wickham appears poor and deserving. Compared to Darcy, he seems the perfect gentleman. He's sociable; he doesn't look down on everyone the way Darcy does; he's careful not to offend.

But this kind of love, "arising on a first interview with its object . . . even before two words have been exchanged"[49] ends up being devastatingly wrong for Elizabeth. As she discovers later, Darcy was the one with all the goodness, while devious Wickham had only the appearance of it. Her first impressions failed her horribly. Through Elizabeth, Austen advises us not to jump too quickly into love, not to entirely trust that love-at-first-sight moment.

What we see here is Austen's voice of caution. It's not to be wondered at, really, when you consider that in Austen's day, courting quickly led to an engagement, which quickly led to marriage, which was a permanent state. Divorce was incredibly uncommon. To err in this decision—to be led astray by those perhaps unfaithful first impressions—could sentence one to life-long misery (as Mr. Bennet could attest, with his silly, incapable wife). Thankfully, we have more time now to learn whether we've judged a guy correctly. We aren't expected to marry quickly. But placing too much faith in those first moments can still lead us into years of unhappiness and regret.

Be open to changing your mind.

Austen gives us this lesson through Elizabeth Bennet's story as well. At the dance where Darcy first makes an appearance, he spurns Lizzy in a loud enough voice that she can hear him. "She is tolerable; but not handsome enough to tempt *me*,"[50] he says. So Lizzy immediately (and understandably, in my opinion) turns against him. His having the great fault of not at once sensing her beauty (he had not yet felt the power of her "fine eyes"[51]) makes her capable of believing every bad thing about him. She promises her mother "*never* to dance with him."[52]

When Elizabeth breaks that promise and dances with Darcy at the Netherfield ball, Charlotte Lucas tells her, "I dare say you will find him very agreeable." Lizzy replies, "Heaven forbid!—*That* would be the greatest misfortune of all!—To find a man agreeable whom one is determined to hate!—Do not wish me such an evil."[53] Yet that is the very "evil" for which Lizzy is destined—to find out that Darcy is not only agreeable, but also even worthy of her. When she truly understands his character, she loves him. She could never have imagined that she would end up marrying him.

Like Lizzy, we may have to face the evil of finding a man agreeable whom we have "determined to hate." Austen would want us to be open to changing our minds, humbling and difficult as that might be, and to be more careful about setting our hearts against someone in the first place. Can you imagine what Lizzy would have missed had she stubbornly held on to her hatred for Darcy?

DON'T LET YOUR VANITY BLIND YOU.

Austen has one more lesson for us from *Pride and Prejudice,* which gets straight to Elizabeth's heart. In her evening prayer Austen wrote, "Save us from deceiving ourselves by pride or vanity."[54] Elizabeth, the character perhaps most like Austen, with her lively wit and spirit, suffers this deception. Vanity, ego—this is at the center of the story. Elizabeth's problem isn't just that her first impressions were all wrong, though they were. It's not just that she has to be willing to change her mind. Through the course of the story, she's forced to recognize deeper faults.

After his first proposal is so strongly rejected, Darcy writes to Elizabeth to explain what she believes are his grievous sins—the way he separated his friend Bingley from her sister Jane and his horrible treatment of Wickham, in not giving him the church living he should have received. The truth is not what Elizabeth wants it to be. At first, she can only contradict everything Darcy says. "This must be false! This cannot be!"[55] she thinks as she reads. But over the two hours she walks in the grounds at Rosings Park rereading Darcy's letter, she comes to entirely different conclusions. Not only does she question her assumptions about Darcy and Wickham, but—more painfully—she questions her own conduct.

Her worst realization is that she, who prides herself on being able to ferret out the truth in people's characters, has gotten these two men entirely wrong, and that she owes this grave mistake entirely to her vanity. Austen shares Lizzy's horror at the discovery:

> *I, who have prided myself on my discernment!—I, who have valued myself on my abilities! . . . How humiliating is this discovery!—Yet, how just a humiliation!—Had I been in love, I could not have been more wretchedly blind! But vanity, not love, has been my folly.—Pleased with the preference of one, and offended by the neglect of the other, on the very beginning of our acquaintance, I have courted prepossession and ignorance, and driven reason away, where either were concerned.*[56]

Everyone liked Wickham and he chose Lizzy, which flattered her. That colored her opinion of him. Unpopular Darcy, averse to anything resembling flattery and too shy to dance, set Lizzy against him from the beginning.

Lizzy's final lesson for us about love—and Austen's, through her—would be that the guy who gives us the most attention, who is the most popular, who flatters our vanity, isn't necessarily the best for us. It pays to be willing to examine our own motivations. If vanity or pride is leading our hearts, it may lead us in the wrong direction.

Make your own decisions.

As Austen learned firsthand, our friends don't always know who will be best for us and may pick the wrong guy. The year after Jane's flirtation with Tom, her dear friend Anne Lefroy decided to invite another possible suitor for the Christmas holidays. Reverend Samuel Blackall had studied at Cambridge and was set to receive a lucrative church living. Financially, he would have been an eligible match for Jane—not too high or too low. Unfortunately, he was also not the least bit attractive to Jane. Austen biographer Deirdre Le Faye writes of "his pompous manner and loud didactic conversation,"[57] which reminds me of the bumbling Mr. Collins. Austen called him "a peice [*sic*] of Perfection, noisy Perfection himself."[58] Even if he was the choice of her friend, Austen could never have loved or married Samuel Blackall. Without any interest on her part, this little attempt at matchmaking quickly died away. When it came to love, Austen made her own decisions.

Another precious source of Austen's thoughts on love comes in the form of letters to her niece Fanny. Fanny's mother died when she was fifteen, and as Fanny was navigating love and marriage in her early twenties, she turned to her Aunt Jane for advice. (Can you imagine being able to write to *that* Aunt Jane for advice on your love life?) Fanny was agonizing about her affections for one John Plumptre. Fanny had known him for a couple of years and had thought she really loved him, only to have that love wane. When Fanny asked Jane her opinion about whom she should marry, Jane hesitated to give an answer, afraid of guiding Fanny in the wrong direction. She replied, "Your own feelings & none but your own, should determine such an important point."[59]

This is also Anne Elliot's lesson in *Persuasion,* although it takes her longer to learn than it did Austen. When Anne was nineteen, she met the dashing Captain Wentworth, just back from a naval victory in the Caribbean. Austen describes him as "a remarkably fine young man, with a great deal of intelligence, spirit and brilliancy"; when he met pretty Anne, they were "rapidly and deeply in love."[60] He proposed, but their great happiness didn't last.

Anne's father, who valued people only by rank, saw nothing of value in the match, so he greeted it with coldness and silence. A mere naval captain was of no interest to him and could bring no value to the family. Anne could have borne her father's disapproval, but not her dear friend Lady Russell's. Following Anne's mother's death years before, Lady Russell had become like a mother to Anne. So when Lady Russell took every opportunity to oppose the match as strongly as she could, Anne could not withstand her persuasion. To Lady Russell's mind, Anne would have been throwing herself away on a young man with only confidence on his side—no fortune, no connections, no guarantee that Anne would not end up poor with a houseful of children, having completely lost her place in society.

Anne broke off the engagement, convinced she was doing the right thing both for herself and for Captain Wentworth. Though their whole acquaintance had lasted just a few months, her heart hurt for years afterward, and as a consequence she suffered "an early loss of bloom and spirits."[61] She never met a man who could compare to Frederick Wentworth. Anne believed, in spite of all its challenges, that she would have been happier had she kept the engagement.

When Captain Wentworth shows up again eight years later (now secure in his fortune), Anne is stronger and less susceptible to being persuaded against him. She knows his character, knows that she still loves him. In spite of the arrival of the family heir—Mr. Elliot—and in spite of Lady Russell's championing Mr. Elliot and continued disdain for Captain Wentworth, Anne makes her own decision.

There's one scene in which Anne visits her old friend Mrs. Smith in Westgate Buildings. Anne tells her that in spite of everyone's expectations, "I am not going to marry Mr. Elliot."[62] This is a statement of power for Anne. For all the things she could not control, she would in fact control who she would marry, in spite of what everyone else in her life attempted to pressure her into.

In our age, we get to control so many things—where we study, what we study, what jobs we take, where we live. It may sound strange to our independent, modern ears, but I think it bears repeating: While friends and family may guide us, and sometimes have wisdom to offer about our choice of man, the decision about whom to love is entirely our own. When our future happiness depends largely on this decision, we are the ones most qualified to make it.

Build love on the foundation of esteem.

Here again is a concept that makes us realize our distance from Austen. *Esteem* may not be much in use today, but for Austen, love could not exist without it. Imitating Austen herself, her characters want to evaluate a man and find out, can they esteem him? Is he worthy of their respect, their admiration? Without that, they could never love.

For this reason, in *Sense and Sensibility* we find thoughtful Elinor talking about Edward's "sense and his goodness . . . The excellence of his understanding and his principles . . . his solid worth." Elinor goes on to explain that she "greatly esteem[s]" Edward, which makes Marianne burst forth: "Cold-hearted Elinor!"[63] For romantic Marianne, esteem held little value. It's also why, when Edward decides to go through with his engagement to Lucy Steele, Elinor "gloried in his integrity."[64] This is the engagement that has separated her from Edward, but if he had chosen to break his word to Lucy, Elinor could never have loved him. His unfaithfulness to Lucy would have been such a fault in his character that Elinor could not have overlooked it.

In *Pride and Prejudice* we find Elizabeth mulling over Darcy's character after discovering that he was the one who searched out Wickham and Lydia in London, and the one who bore all the cost of discharging Wickham's debts and making him marry Lydia. "For herself she was humbled," Austen tells us of Elizabeth, "but she was proud of him. Proud that in a cause of compassion and honour, he had been able to get the better of himself."[65]

Lizzy's heart had already turned to loving Darcy, dating back (as she jokes) to the day she saw his fine grounds at Pemberley. But it was the intelligence the housekeeper gave that day that turned Lizzy's heart in his favor. The old servant fairly glows as she talks of her master. She describes him as kindhearted and good-natured, a giving brother who would do anything for his sister, and the best landlord. Like his father before him, he is kind to the poor. Elizabeth recognizes that she may have been wrong in characterizing him as all arrogance and pride, and with the knowledge that he may in fact be worthy of her esteem, her love begins to grow.

Persuasion's Captain Wentworth, as well, loves Anne not only because she is pretty but because "Her character was now fixed on his mind as perfection itself, maintaining the loveliest medium of fortitude and gentleness." He tries, but can't find anyone to equal Anne. That's one of the reasons Austen gives for Wentworth and Anne being even happier the second time they are engaged—they are "more fixed in a knowledge of each other's character," so they are "more exquisitely happy."[66]

Through all of this, Austen reminds us of the more serious, more thoughtful nature of love. She asks us to recognize that when we bind ourselves to someone, the quality of his character will be in large part what gives us happiness or, conversely, pain. It sounds terribly old-fashioned compared to our standards, which tend to be centered on how a guy makes us feel, if we find him attractive, or whether or not he makes us laugh. If anything, though, Austen wants to make sure we get all those things we want, in the form of a good man who will treat us well for years to come.

Be realistic.

This is not the advice we expect from Austen. After all, what does romance have to do with reality? For Austen, though, love is firmly grounded, not quite as dreamy a thing as we may think, as she shows us in the story of Henry Tilney and Catherine Morland in *Northanger Abbey*. By the time Henry proposes, he is "sincerely attached to" Catherine, and "felt and delighted in all the excellencies of her character and truly loved her society." Austen admits, though, that "his affection originated in nothing better than gratitude, or, in other words, that a persuasion of her partiality for him had been the only cause of giving her a serious thought."[67] Henry began thinking about Catherine because he knew she liked him—perhaps not as dramatic as befitted a romantic heroine, Austen jokes, but Austen wrote as she found in life. She knew that love could be real and lasting without being desperately romantic.

DON'T EVER THINK YOU'RE TOO OLD TO HOPE FOR LOVE.

This is my favorite of Austen's lessons on love—you are never too old to hope. It makes me think that she continued to hope for herself. Elizabeth Elliot in *Persuasion* feels herself approaching "the years of danger"[68] at twenty-nine. Marianne Dashwood in *Sense and Sensibility* declares that "A woman of seven and twenty can never hope to feel or inspire affection again," and supposes that any marriage such an old woman would make would merely be "a compact of convenience,"—she would provide "the offices of a nurse, for the sake of the provision and security of a wife."[69] What a horrible picture! But to counteract all this ageism, Austen gives us the story of Anne Elliot. In spite of losing her bloom early because of her disappointment at nineteen with Captain Wentworth, Anne goes on to be sought by not one, but two men, to regain her spirit and all of her good looks, and to be proposed to at the (then) very old age of twenty-eight, marrying not just anyone, but the love of her life, the only man she could ever imagine loving.

Austen would tell us that there is no deadline, no age limit, no time after which we may presume that love will never find us. One advantage we have over the eighteenth century is that those "years of danger" that Elizabeth Elliot feared have been pushed back much later in life, if not disappeared entirely. We have no need to feel rushed into marriage in order to secure our future but can wait until we really know who we are and what we want in a partner. Austen herself never seems to have felt pressured, in spite of the expectations of the era. Even if she never married, I would doubt that she ever entirely gave up hope.

Embrace the mystery.

One of the things that comes through clearly in Austen's letters to her niece Fanny is the fact that no matter how much Austen analyzed love, she still respected the fact that it was essentially mysterious. Writing to Fanny about Mr. John Plumptre, Austen agrees that Fanny "cannot be in Love. . . . What strange creatures we are!" she says. "It seems as if your being secure of him (as you say yourself) had made you Indifferent."[70] Austen believes that Fanny thought she loved Mr. Plumptre because he was the first man ever to pursue her, but her strange and fickle heart, now certain of his affection, has decided she may not really want him.

In the first half of the letter, Austen encourages Fanny to try to fall back in love with Mr. Plumptre, listing all of his wonderful qualities: "His situation in life, family, friends, & above all his Character—his uncommonly amiable mind, strict principles, just notions, good habits." In Austen's eyes, "His only fault indeed seems Modesty" and taking life and religion perhaps a bit too seriously. As Austen writes, "the warmer my feelings become," she says, "the more strongly I feel the sterling worth of such a young Man & the desirableness of your growing in love with him again. I recommend this most thoroughly."[71]

Then Austen completely changes her tone: "And now, my dear Fanny, having written so much on one side of the question, I shall turn round & entreat you not to commit yourself farther, & not to think of accepting him unless you really do like him . . . if his deficiencies of Manner . . . strike you more than all his good qualities, if you continue to think strongly of them, give him up at once."[72]

Austen knew, regardless of the worth of the man in question, regardless of how much we perhaps *should* like him, we just might not. Yes, "What strange creatures we are!" And what a mystery is love—enough of a mystery that Austen herself was not always able to see clearly the right answer, was forced to deliberate both sides of the question. Austen would most likely tell us what she told Fanny, "how capable you are . . . of being really in love."[73] She knew that love does not always strictly adhere to reason. We must wait for someone we "really do like," and liking—loving—is at times a mysterious, inscrutable thing.

Chapter 4

Pursuing Passion

Jane Austen never had sex. (Perhaps nothing I could say would shock you more.) As much as you may want to imagine her sneaking off with Tom Lefroy for something passionate, that didn't happen. Her fate was no different than the average eighteenth-century woman who never married. Sex was just not part of her life.

This may sound inexplicable to you, but there are reasons for it. First, Austen's Christian faith taught her that sex should be reserved for marriage. Her faith was important to her; she wanted to live it out rather than just talk about it. She would have wanted to be faithful even—or perhaps especially—with her sexuality. Second, birth control was for all practical purposes unavailable, and there was no protection for a woman who had sex before or outside of marriage. If she got pregnant, or even if she was just discovered to have had sex, she would have been a social outcast with no hope and no future. One fling had the very real potential to ruin her life forever.

In one letter commenting on friends who had just had their eighteenth child, Austen recommends "the simple regimen of separate rooms"[74] for the parents—advising the married couple to simply abstain from sex to prevent future pregnancies. Today we might wonder at the naiveté Austen conveys with those words. It seems she not only didn't have sex, but may not have understood the depth of passion and the difficulty a married couple may have had abstaining. (Although after eighteen children, perhaps abstinence would have been a welcome relief.)

If the whole world has changed in the 230-plus years since Austen was born, I can't imagine anything that's changed more than our attitudes and actions in regard to sex. What was then in large part (with exceptions, of course) saved for marriage is now extremely casual. The sexual pictures on our billboards, in our magazines, the sex in TV shows and movies—Austen wouldn't be able to imagine a world like this. She also would not be able to imagine birth control and the freedom it provides. So what can an eighteenth-century virgin possibly teach us about sex? What guidance could she have to offer?

Know this: The guy who wants to sleep with you may not love you.

Coming from the perspective of more than 200 years ago, it's no surprise that much of what Austen has to say about sex is cautionary. And as much as we can talk about the differences between the eighteenth and twenty-first centuries, some things never change. It's been said that girls give sex to get love, and guys give love to get sex. Austen knew this from watching the world around her, and knew that nothing could be more irresistible or more devastating for a woman than to be seduced by a man who seemed to love her.

This is apparent in *Sense and Sensibility* in the story of Colonel Brandon's ward, Eliza. He takes great care in her upbringing, but at seventeen she goes to Bath with a friend whose father is ill, leaving the girls largely unsupervised. Here Eliza meets Willoughby and falls madly in love with him, believing he feels the same way about her. She runs away with Willoughby, but after several months his love has vanished and she is pregnant. He leaves her alone with no money and no idea of his whereabouts, saying he will write but never again contacting her. Brandon finally hears from her shortly before she is to give birth. Her fate is tragic: She will be excluded from society, raising the child of a man who took her heart but never really loved her.

Lydia in *Pride and Prejudice* also fell for this. She flirted incessantly with Wickham, and when he proposed an elopement, she believed he would marry her (although she wasn't terribly particular about when that marriage took place). What Wickham really wanted, though, was to sleep with Lydia, to enjoy her company for a while and then leave when she became tiresome. Austen says Lydia and Wickham had little hope of happiness, only being together "because their passions were stronger than their virtue."[75] But Lydia was comparatively one of the lucky ones. Darcy bribed Wickham to actually go through with the marriage.

As little happiness as the Wickhams must have had, Lydia was still able to have a life. When she and her army husband arrived in their northern regiment, they could have gone on as though nothing unseemly had happened.

To a modern woman in an age where hookups are commonplace, it may seem quaint to tell you that guys will feign love to get sex. But Austen reminds us—love and sex aren't necessarily the same thing.

Don't expect the world to be fair to women.

The eighteenth century was incredibly unfair to women, as Austen shows us in her stories. Willoughby's abandoned lover Eliza, for example, has no hope of a life, will never have the chance to love anyone else, and will never be respectable. She will be isolated and alone for as long as she lives. But Willoughby gets to go on as though nothing happened—as though he's not the scoundrel who helped create Eliza's desperate situation. He marries well, has plenty of money, and lives a life of leisure in the best society. His wealthy cousin even forgives him, so that he is not disinherited after all.

Austen provides an even worse example in the form of Eliza's mother. She had been secretly engaged to Colonel Brandon but was forced to marry his older brother, who abused her. Cruelly treated and miserable, with no hope of happiness, she strayed.

Her lover abandoned her; her husband divorced her and kept her money for himself. So she sank further and further. The impression we get from Brandon's story is that she sunk as low as a woman could go, forced to do whatever she could to earn a living. She ended up in debtor's prison and died of consumption.

In Austen's time, a man could do just about anything, but a woman who made one mistake—however justified—might never be forgiven, paying for her sins in the worst possible way. Austen would rejoice to find our modern world so different, and so should we. Still, men and women may never be entirely equal here. In the realm of sex, a woman always risks more. A man will never have to carry an unplanned pregnancy and make the difficult, life-altering decisions that entails. He also generally doesn't bring the same emotional vulnerability to sexual encounters. Thank God we don't have to live in Austen's world, but our own isn't free of inequality.

Think about it.

Beyond extreme shock, there's no telling what Austen's reaction would be to the sexual mores of our day. Would she approve of one-night stands and hooking up? (That's difficult to imagine.) Would she urge chastity? There's no way for us to know. But what I believe we *can* know is that she would want us all to think about what we're doing. Before making decisions about our sexuality, she would want us to understand our motivations—are our standards simply society's standards? If so, which ones? If we have religious faith, what does it teach us? Is sex okay where there's love, and in that case, what do we mean by *love*? Is love a vague, intangible feeling, or does it involve some kind of commitment? What are the potential consequences? In one aspect of our lives that has become increasingly thoughtless, Austen would urge us to think.

Austen has compassion for the women who are seduced by the Willoughbys of the world. Even foolish Lydia Bennet merits some empathy from readers; had her parents molded her character, she could have been so much more. Mr. Collins's suggestion that her family banish Lydia forever and never speak her name again is greeted with the disdain it deserves. Though Lydia never really recognizes the error of her ways, she is forgiven and welcomed home.

Austen has less compassion for Maria Bertram in *Mansfield Park*. With every advantage, Maria remains thoughtless and grasping. She has more than enough money, but marries the distinctly unintelligent Mr. Rushworth—whom she knows she doesn't love—primarily so she can have a fashionable house in town. She flirts with cavalier, dashing Henry Crawford throughout her engagement, and when he reappears after she is married, she runs off with him, hoping to divorce Rushworth and marry Crawford instead. But Henry has no permanent interest in Maria. He doesn't love her; he only wanted to know that he could regain her affections.

Unlike Lydia Bennet, Maria Bertram is not forgiven nor welcomed home. Her horrified father doesn't want to condone her actions or force the rest of the neighborhood to continue to receive her. So he sends Maria off to live in the country, along with her horrible, petty Aunt Norris. There she will live, alone, for the rest of her life, no hope of marriage or anything else. Maria's shame is "a disgrace never to be wiped off"[76]—all of which could have been avoided had she once stopped to consider what she was doing, to contemplate the dangers of marrying a man she never loved and the risk of running off with Henry Crawford.

The eighteenth century in general may not have had great respect for a woman's cognitive capabilities, but Jane Austen did. She believed that a woman's thoughts should guide her actions—especially in matters of sex. For Austen, desires were not to be trusted solely, without the careful chaperoning of the mind.

Allow your heart and your head to rule together.

If we think of Austen as a sort of patron saint of romance, this advice may shock us. For us, love is all about feeling. For her, echoing her guidance about sex, romance itself was as much about thought as about feeling, and involved the mind as well as the heart.

Austen knew that even where no sex was involved, passion might still play the leading role and guide one into error. In *Sense and Sensibility,* Marianne is nothing but feeling and imagination (the *sensibility* of the title). She despises Elinor's self-command, sees no value in it, and instead of guiding her feelings, she feeds them, in order to experience them to the fullest.

This affects all of Marianne's life—when her father dies, she is inconsolable, incapable of exerting herself. When forced to leave Barton Park, she mourns for all the trees and the views she will never see again. She is, in general, never willing to do anything she doesn't *feel* like doing—especially when it involves being civil to people she doesn't like.

But, most of all, this affects Marianne's love life. When handsome Willoughby finds her having twisted her ankle in a rainstorm, her romantic heart is quickly his. Here is the man she had given up hope of ever meeting. He "enter[s] into all [her] feelings,"[77]—he loves the same music, the same poetry. Guided by emotion, Marianne ventures into all kinds of impropriety, ignoring just about everyone for Willoughby's sake, even going to take a tour of Willoughby's cousin's estate with only Willoughby as her company, without an invitation from the cousin—viewing her future home, as it were.

Marianne believes her feelings could never fail her, never guide her wrong. When she realizes just how wrong she has been—when Willoughby leaves her without explanation, ignores her letters, and becomes engaged to Miss Grey, with her £50,000 fortune—Marianne simply exchanges one set of feelings for another. Grief replaces happiness, and just the same, knows no limits. The misery she encourages affects her so deeply that her body is weakened, and when she becomes ill, she nearly dies.

Marianne recognizes later the extent to which giving supremacy to her emotions has been a grave error: "Had I died," she says, "it would have been self-destruction." She compares her conduct to "what it ought to have been"[78]—to Elinor's. Throughout the novel, Elinor loves and grieves as well, but her feelings have been moderated, not only by reason but by a desire to spare her family pain.

While Elinor's approach may seem a bit severe, Marianne is no doubt convinced of its merits by the end of the story. Had she approached Willoughby with a little less romantic feeling and a little more thought, she might have contemplated the possibility of his aunt's disapproval before she planned to be mistress of his estates. She would not have assumed his love for her before he stated it, would not have presumed an engagement that didn't exist. She would have been more able to recognize and share her sister's grief, and may have been able to spare her family the agony of seeing her nearly die.

If Marianne could advise us, she would ask us to enter into romance with our heads as well as our hearts.

Recognize that love can be both passionate fire and gentle flame.

Austen's heroines marry for love. Anne Elliot is so in love with her Captain Wentworth that she believes that regardless of what happens, whether he proposes or not, she could never love anyone else. And it's hard to imagine Elizabeth and Darcy's relationship being tepid. But Austen gives us a different perspective with the ending of Marianne Dashwood's story, which makes me think that Austen understood that passion could appear in different forms. What we tend to see as overwhelming emotion, she saw as also steady and gentle.

Marianne begins the story completely devoted to romance, but at the end she marries Colonel Brandon "with no sentiment superior to strong esteem and lively friendship." Austen does not give us the prospect of a loveless Marianne, however. "Marianne could never love by halves," she tells us, "and her whole heart became, in time, as much devoted to her husband, as it had once been to Willoughby."[79] For Austen, this more gentle love could prove to be just as fulfilling as that begun with a surfeit of romantic feeling.

Austen wrote comparatively little about passion and sex, but what we hear from her over the space of the two hundred years separating us is largely a voice of caution and restraint—perhaps unsurprisingly. We can't draw out any specific dos and don'ts that apply to modern life, but she urges us to use our minds even in this emotion-charged realm and not to allow any form of desire to hold supremacy over careful thought. Maybe it's impossible to separate Austen from the eighteenth century, to imagine her any less devoted to reason and more to heedless passion. (Although even in the eighteenth century there was heedless passion to be had, as she knew.) Certainly she would find every opportunity to skewer our sexual obsessions, as much as they have the potential to make us ridiculous. Perhaps her common-sense guidance can prove to be a helpful corrective in our overly sexed world.

Chapter 5

Finding a Good Man

Jane Austen loved to admire men and also loved to joke about them—which is pretty much how she approached all of life. She found them horrid or delightful, and spoke as she found them. She wanted them to be enthusiastic about literature, not to be taciturn and dour but to talk—as long as they didn't talk too much. And she was especially partial to a pair of "beautiful dark eyes."[80] At twenty-three she teased a Mr. Calland into dancing at a ball, describing him as "altogether rather the Genius & Flirt of the Evening."[81] A little genius and a little flirtation would always have been welcome to Jane—conceit and insincerity, on the other hand, would not be accepted. Of Fanny's beau John Plumptre, she wrote, "I set him down as sensible rather than Brilliant.—There is nobody Brilliant nowadays."[82] Her brother Henry's doctor, Mr. Haden—more of an age for her niece Fanny than for Jane herself—she found "something between a Man & an Angel,"[83] with his "good Manners & clever conversation."[84] She would have thought that a man who was witty, thoughtful, and literary had been blessed with the "gifts of Fortune."[85]

How would she advise us in our own search? Austen, of course, would understand the appeal of a good-looking guy worth 10,000 pounds a year (the modern-day equivalent of a seven-figure salary), but what would she tell us if she could guide us toward our own Mr. Darcy, our own "Man & Angel"?

Look for a good guy.

By this point, we know that Jane wants us to find a good guy—a good-hearted guy, someone who will treat us and others well. She would think we were fools if we didn't look beyond physical appearance and money and all the other surface-y things to the more important substance underneath. She wrote jokingly of family friend Mr. Digweed: "Handsome is as Handsome does; he is therefore a very ill-looking Man."[86] We know, too, that first impressions may lead us horribly wrong, that someone who appears good and decent may in fact be malicious and awful. (Wickham or Willoughby, anyone?) The saving grace for many of Austen's characters was that they discovered the true nature of these less-than-worthy men before committing to them.

Although you may find a different caliber of men at a bar versus a service project, finding a good guy doesn't have so much to do with where we look as much as how we look. It's about our attitude toward dating, about striving to know someone at a deeper level, to know who he is (e.g., thoughtful, humble) rather than just what he is (good-looking, well-educated). It's about being impressed by substantive things like the way he interacts with those beneath him or how he relates to his family, about seeing how he treats you over time. I doubt Austen would condemn online dating, or any other method of meeting, but she might find it a forum in which it's easy to allow superficial things pre-eminence—to rule someone in or out based solely on the quality of a photograph. (Then again, she'd probably find some profiles and pictures pricelessly ridiculous, an apt target for her rapier wit.)

Jane's characters may have had some advantages over us, in that they lived in a more connected society. Elizabeth learns about Wickham's attempted elopement with Georgiana Darcy precisely because she knows Darcy, and appeals to him (or rather insults him), thereby discovering the actual truth of the situation. Darcy and Wickham, as much as they detest each other, are connected in the small country society that Elizabeth is part of. Anne Elliot in *Persuasion* discovers Mr. Elliot's true character in part because he used to be a close friend of her close friend Mrs. Smith.

As much as these associations may have been carefully constructed by the author, it seems as if it would have been easier to find those connections in that society, to actually know people who know the guy you might be dating, to get some background on him. In our day, when we meet someone online who lives hours away, our resources are more limited. True, we have Google, and I'm sure Jane would approve of Google-stalking. (A girl has to attempt to find the dirt if it's there, right?) But I think her greatest advice to us would be to keep our eyes open and watch carefully, to not commit too quickly before we really understand a guy's character.

There are some women who seem to enjoy dating bad guys, for whom good guys are just boring. (True, some good guys may be boring, but not the ones of whom Austen would approve.) Austen wrote of one acquaintance, "Miss Jackson is married to young Mr Gunthorpe, & is to be very unhappy. He swears, drinks, is cross, jealous, selfish & Brutal."[87] I've never understood the Miss Jacksons of the world, simply because "the jealous, selfish & Brutal" type will eventually direct that brutality at you. When your happiness depends in large part on the nature of the person you're with—as it still does these days, no matter how different our lives are in other ways—you want to make sure that guy is a good guy.

Look for a good-looking guy.

Don't worry—Jane isn't so concerned with moral character that she's forgotten about other important (even if more superficial) things. As Lizzy Bennet says of Mr. Bingley, "He is also handsome, which a young man ought likewise to be, if he possibly can."[88] Austen would agree; a man should try to be handsome in addition to being good. If Mr. Bingley is allowed to be handsome, Mr. Darcy is described as "fine" and "tall," with "handsome features, noble mien."[89] It's impossible to imagine Darcy any other way—whichever movie version you happen to love best. And Anne's Captain Wentworth was "a remarkably fine young man, with a great deal of intelligence, spirit, and brilliancy."[90] Dashing, indeed.

But it's not so much about good looks as it is about finding someone you have a spark with, someone who is attractive to you for whatever reason. Some of Austen's characters are not quite so good-looking on first acquaintance but are acknowledged to become so once you get to know them. Elinor, in *Sense and Sensibility,* describes her Edward Ferrars: "At first sight, his address is certainly not striking; and his person can hardly be called handsome, till the expression of his eyes, which are uncommonly good, and the general sweetness of his countenance, is perceived. At present, I know him so well, that I think him really handsome; or, at least, almost so."[91] If Edward's goodness made him more appealing, Henry Crawford in *Mansfield Park* is aided by his devilish cunning and spirit—and his good teeth:

> *Her brother [Henry Crawford] was not handsome; no, when they first saw him he was absolutely plain, black and plain; but still he was the gentleman, with a pleasing address. The second meeting proved him not so very plain; he was plain, to be sure, but then he had so much countenance, and his teeth were so good, and he was so well made, that one soon forgot he was plain . . .*[92]

Edward Ferrars's deficiencies don't keep Elinor from falling deeply in love with him, and Henry Crawford, however plain he may have looked on first appearance, nearly wins over Fanny Price and ultimately proves to be so strong a temptation as to draw Maria Bertram away from her admittedly not-good-looking husband.

It's been acknowledged for a long time that women are capable of this—of finding a guy more attractive the better they know him. What I love about Austen is that she gives us an example of a man doing the same, finding a woman better looking than he initially thought. She writes of Darcy, "No sooner had he made it clear to himself and his friends that [Elizabeth] had hardly a good feature in her face, than he began to find it was rendered uncommonly intelligent by the beautiful expression of her dark eyes."[93] Austen would remind us that even our impressions of someone's appearance may change with time.

Look for the guy who is right for you.

In spite of all of the above, it's possible that you will meet a guy of sterling character and good looks and simply not love him. In this case, Jane would tell you to move on, and look for the one who is right for you. In her letters to her niece Fanny, who is wondering what to do about the wonderful if somewhat too serious John Plumptre, she gives her just this advice. "It is very true that you never may attach another Man, his equal altogether," she says, "but if that other Man has the power of attaching you *more*, he will be in your eyes the most perfect."[94]

As Austen acknowledges, love is, after all, a matter of personal taste, and the guy who seems perfect to me may not seem so to you.

Expect the unexpected.

Many of us have in our minds an idea of what this man—"the one"—will be like, the kind of movies and music he'll like, the kind of work he'll do, what he will look like, what will make him laugh. In fact, many of us have a mental checklist of what we think we need in the right man. Yet with all of these expectations, one of Austen's lessons for us about love is this: Prepare to be surprised.

Elinor met Edward during one of the darkest periods of her life, just after her father's death, when surely, of all things she may have been expecting, she wouldn't have been expecting to fall in love. And if she had anticipated falling in love, it wouldn't have been with the brother of her stingy and pretentious sister-in-law. Marianne, who initially believes you can only really love once, spends that precious young love on Willoughby. She would never have believed it if someone told her she would eventually marry and give her whole heart to the Colonel. Emma strongly believes she will never marry but ends up desperately loving Mr. Knightley, a dear friend and almost a brother to her, who is almost twice her age and who held her as a baby.

If we try to predict love, we will likely fail. Love may be the farthest thing from our minds when the right guy finally walks in. If we become arrogant or too sure of what we believe will happen, we are destined to be humbled. Unexpected love may grow out of a long-term friendship, or we may fall in love with someone we once thought was far too old (or far too young), or we may simply fall in love with someone who is the opposite of everything we thought we wanted or needed but who turns out to be our *just right*. As much as we can plan what we're looking for, when we finally find the right man, he may come as a shock, completely challenging our expectations.

Don't worry about having standards that are too high.

If there's one thing my friends and I have wondered from time to time throughout our dating years, it's this: Are our standards too high? Austen would encourage us to keep those standards high and perhaps even make them higher.

Sometimes I'm shocked at how much Austen required in a man. One of the passages that always strikes me is from *Persuasion,* when Anne is considering the character of Mr. Elliot and beginning to find fault in it. After a month, Anne finds him to be "a sensible man, an agreeable man,—that he talked well, professed good opinions, seemed to judge properly and as a man of principle . . . nor could she fix on any one article of moral duty evidently transgressed . . ." But Anne struggles to believe that all these good things about Mr. Elliot are actually true. She fears what he was in the past, knows that "there had been bad habits," wonders if he has really changed, if "his mind was truly cleansed."

Then Anne goes on to give a more thorough critique of Mr. Elliot's manners, and this is the part that always gets me:

> *Mr. Elliot was rational, discreet, polished,—but he was not open. There was never any burst of feeling, any warmth of indignation or delight, at the evil or good of others. This, to Anne, was a decided imperfection. . . . She felt that she could so much more depend upon the sincerity of those who sometimes looked or said a careless or a hasty thing, than of those whose presence of mind never varied, whose tongue never slipped.*

Mr. Elliot was too generally agreeable. Various as were the tempers in her father's house, he pleased them all. . . . He had spoken to her with some degree of openness of Mrs. Clay; had appeared completely to see what Mrs. Clay was about, and to hold her in contempt; and yet Mrs. Clay found him as agreeable as anybody.[95]

In the first paragraph, Anne worries about the fact that Mr. Elliot doesn't express himself openly enough, that perhaps he isn't entirely sincere. In the second, Anne is worried that he is popular with everyone, that he is too well-liked, even by those with whom he finds fault. She seems to be holding him to impossibly high standards.

In both of these cases, though, Anne's intuition was working, and she would be justified in her opinions later when she learned the true nature of Mr. Elliot's black heart. He was not open with her because he wasn't showing his true self, only playing a game, making sure that he never revealed his true character and only presenting what would have been acceptable to Anne. And he was too well-liked because he played different parts to different people. If he convinced Anne that he found fault with Mrs. Clay, at the same time, he was convincing Mrs. Clay to become his mistress. So Anne's—and Austen's—standards appear justified, but at first they certainly seem too high.

If Austen wouldn't have us lower our standards, she would have us examine them and make sure that our high standards are the right ones. Marianne's standards are high enough, but she finds out that they're fairly if not entirely wrong. She wants someone who shares all of her passions, who loves the same books and the same music, who sees the world exactly the way she does. She's horrified that Edward doesn't love drawing the same way Elinor does, and only hopes that maybe he will be inspired to take it up so that they will share this love. Marianne finds what she has always wanted in Willoughby, but his love of the same books and music doesn't save him from being a cad, or make him the right guy for her.

So if you've been building a list—a long list—of all the things you want to find in common with someone, of what he will wear and do and read and listen to, Austen would probably encourage you to re-examine that list, to make sure that your high standards are focused largely on matters of greater importance. And should you meet a guy who exceeds all of your standards, provided you don't see warning signs the way Anne Elliot did, don't let him go. As Austen tells us in *Mansfield Park*, "nobody minds having what is too good for them."[96]

Don't get too caught up in the idea of "the one."

Today, more than in Austen's day, we obsess about finding "the one"—the one right guy who is meant for us, the only guy we'll be happy with. How would Jane feel about that? Well, I think it's complicated.

The only character in Austen's novels who espouses something similar is Marianne, who believes you can only love once. For Marianne, a first love is the only love, and a "second attachment"[97] is unthinkable. Regardless of what happens with that first love, whether it's successful or tragic, Marianne doesn't think anyone capable of truly loving again, which may explain why she is so devastatingly lost after Willoughby breaks her heart. In her mind, it's not just the end of her relationship with Willoughby, but the end of love, period. If there's no such thing as second attachments, Marianne has no hope of ever loving again. Thankfully, she lives to prove herself wrong.

I'm tempted to say that Austen would find our idea of "the one" foolish. I think she would tell us that if you meet a good guy whom you love, then you have indeed found the one for you and should stop obsessing about whether or not he could be the one person in the universe that you were destined for. At times we marry someone we love, someone who seems to be "the one," only to change our minds later when that romantic love becomes the stuff of the more mundane everyday. Then, we may set off again to find someone who this time might *really* be the one, and start all over with him. Jane would have no part of that, I'm sure.

And when it comes to whether there's actually only one right guy for us, or whether there are many possibilities, I think Jane would come down on the side of there being many possibilities. But there are a few things in her writing that give me pause. For one, she encourages her niece Fanny to wait until she meets the man who is "in [her] eyes the most perfect,"[98]—the guy who is right for her, who kind of sounds like our idea of "the one."

Then there's Elinor. When she learns that Edward will marry Lucy Steele, and when she's finally able to talk about this with Marianne, she presents a strong, stoic front. With time, she expects

Edward—and we can assume, also herself—to be able to be happy. "And after all, Marianne," she says, "after all that is bewitching in the idea of a single and constant attachment, and all that can be said of one's happiness depending entirely on any particular person, it is not meant—it is not fit—it is not possible that it should be so."[99]

Yet however well Elinor paints the picture of all that both she and Edward have to support them, as readers, we know that there's no way Edward could ever be content with Lucy Steele, not after having loved Elinor, and that Elinor, in spite of all her "constant and painful exertion"[100] to try to feel differently, will always regret him. In the end, Austen seems to agree with us, because the book ends the only way that could make us happy: with Edward and Elinor together.

With her reasonable mind, Austen may object to our idea of "the one," or at least to the extreme to which we sometimes carry that idea. But with her heart, I think she might sympathize.

Be the right woman.

There's talk in some circles today about the fact that if you want to attract the right man, you need to be the right woman—in other words, if you're looking for a good guy, you need to make sure that you're the kind of woman he would want. Austen would concur.

Emma illustrates this point best. Emma had to be willing to take Mr. Knightley's reproach—to be humbled, to learn that she had character flaws, that she could be cruel and that all her conceits about matchmaking only ended in a big mess. Her contrition makes him "[look] at her with a glow of regard."[101] Indeed, Emma's manner of accepting Mr. Knightley's rebuke may have been the stroke that made him realize he loved her. "I have blamed you, and lectured you, and you have borne it as no other woman in England would have borne it,"[102] he tells her.

How much better for us if there would be no confrontation, no need to be humbled and set right. Austen would tell us, I'm sure, that if we have terribly high standards for the man we are looking for, we need to make sure, first, that we're living up to those standards ourselves. She would want us to have Lizzy's wit blended with her sister Jane's goodness, to have Marianne's romantic nature held in check with Elinor's careful sense, and to have the kindness Emma developed. She would tell us, too, that when we are happy with our own character and have no need to be ashamed of our own thoughts and actions, *that* itself would be a great source of happiness, even should the right man *not* come along.

While Austen would want us to make ourselves better, she would never want us to change for a man—which may be what we're tempted to do and is a different thing entirely. She wouldn't ever have wanted Elinor to give up drawing just because Edward didn't have an aptitude for it, or for Lizzy to stop dancing because Darcy wasn't so fond of it. She would want us to be gracefully and happily ourselves, and to find someone (to quote *Bridget Jones's Diary*) who loves us just the way we are—which may be that much more likely when we're being who we were meant to be.

Do not be in a hurry.

One thing Austen makes clear (if it wasn't clear enough already from our own experiences) is that when it comes to men, we have absolutely no control over timing. Remember Anne Elliot from *Persuasion,* who breaks off her engagement with Captain Wentworth at nineteen? He enters her life again almost eight years later, and by the time he proposes, Anne is twenty-eight. In all that time, Anne waited. She never met anyone she valued as highly as Frederick Wentworth, never met any man who could again inspire her to love. (You might even say that he was *the one* for her.) Even after he comes back into Anne's life, she has to wait through his flirtation with Louisa Musgrove, while he stubbornly tries to love anyone but Anne. Sometimes, Austen would tell us, finding the right man requires a great deal of patience and persistence. We are not all (are any of us?) as fortunate as Emma, realizing our love and having everything happily settled within two days.

Austen's niece Fanny eventually decided that she could not marry Mr. John Plumptre and changed her behavior toward him, becoming more cold and distant, so that he would understand that he had no hope of winning her affections. But about two years later, Fanny heard that he was to marry someone else, and she began to regret her decision, to wonder if she had done the right thing. She turned to her Aunt Jane once more for advice.

Jane writes, "Why should you be living in dread of his marrying somebody else?—(Yet, how natural!)—You did not chuse *[sic]* to have him yourself; why not allow him to take comfort where he can?"[103] In her next letter, Jane encourages Fanny:

> *Do not be in a hurry; depend upon it, the right Man will come at last; you will in the course of the next two or three years, meet with somebody more generally unexceptionable than anyone you have yet known, who will love you as warmly as ever* He *did, & who will so completely attach you, that you will feel you never really loved before.*[104]

This encouragement is what so many of us want to hear—"depend upon it, the right Man will come at last." (And he did for Fanny: Seven years later she married Sir Edward Knatchbull, and went on to have nine children.) Alas, we have to take this with a rather unwelcome grain of salt, knowing that the right man never did come for Fanny's beloved Aunt Jane. But I think if Jane were here, she would still encourage us to have hope. And, she would say that when we do meet him, we should cherish him. "There *are* such beings in the World perhaps, one in a Thousand, as the Creature You & I should think perfection," Austen writes, "where Grace & Spirit are united to Worth, where the Manners are equal to the Heart & Understanding."[105]

So when he does come along, remember the value of what you've found.

Chapter 6

Recovering from a Broken Heart

Jane Austen doesn't tell us anything in her letters about the times her heart may have been broken, so we're left to speculate about what happened and how much it hurt her. The only scrap we have about her grief over Tom Lefroy is the one statement to her sister Cassandra, about her "tears flow[ing]"[106] as she thought about his leaving and depriving her of further opportunities to flirt. But she wrote in jest, presumably.

The relationship most likely to have touched Jane's heart is the one that is murkiest, only surviving in a vague story passed down by Cassandra to one of her nieces. It's the story of an unnamed suitor by the seaside. When the Austens were living in Bath after Mr. Austen retired, they often spent time at the Devon and Dorset coasts. On one of these trips, when Jane was in her mid-to-late twenties, the Austens developed a friendship with this unnamed man over a period of several weeks. Hesitant to part ways, he asked where they would be the following summer, with a clear intention to join them. Cassandra thought he loved her sister, that "he was worthy of her," and that the proposal she expected him to give would have been welcomed. By Cassandra's recollection, he was "one so unusually gifted with all that was agreeable."[107] No doubt to catch Jane's heart he would have had wit and intellect and kindness. Tragically, they soon heard that he had died. Whatever possible romance there had been came to a heartbreaking end. We don't know whether he actually did love Jane and whether she returned that love. We don't know if he was planning to propose and if she was planning to accept, but that seems possible—and if so, how deeply she must have felt this devastating blow.

Jane wrote of her brother Henry after his wife died, "his Mind is not a Mind for affliction. He is too Busy, too active, too sanguine."[108] It's a trait that brother and sister seem to have shared. Whatever Jane's heartbreak, I don't believe she would have lingered there unnecessarily long. And whatever that heartbreak was, she mulled it over and wove it into her stories, where she gave us narratives of women walking through this kind of pain.

In this case, though, most of Austen's examples are negative—examples she would rather that we *didn't* emulate. Marianne nearly died when Willoughby broke her heart. Elinor refused to allow herself to express any emotion at all. Jane Bennet pretended rather unsuccessfully to be just fine. Anne Elliot, if she continued dutifully on, lost her bloom, her joy. Through these stories, we can gather what would be Austen's advice for our own hurting hearts.

Don't allow your heart to be broken forever.

One of the most poignant stories of heartbreak comes not from Austen's novels, but from her sister Cassandra's life. While we don't have a definite date, it seems that Jane's beautiful sister became engaged to family friend Tom Fowle in December of 1792, when he was twenty-seven and she was nineteen. Tom would have been well-known to the Austen family, having lived with them as a pupil of Mr. Austen's for four years.

The Austens ran a small school out of their modest home, in addition to Mr. Austen's church work (he served as rector of their local parish in the little village of Steventon) and running a farm. They raised six boys of their own and took in four or five others at a time as students. Mr. Austen had studied at Oxford and was well equipped to teach the boys everything they would need to know to succeed at university. Cassandra would have been very young when Tom was there, and he would have bunked upstairs in the attic with her brothers. He must have seemed like something of a brother to Cassandra and Jane as well. At any rate, they knew each other from the time Cassandra was a child.

Regardless of romance, and however much in love they might have been—and it seems they were much in love—Tom and Cassandra simply couldn't afford to marry. He had been given one small church living by a relative, Lord Craven, who had many more lucrative church livings to give, and who had promised one of these to Tom as soon as it became available. But church livings then were essentially held for life, so no one could really tell when one would be free. Tom and Cassandra were basically waiting for someone to either retire or die so that Tom could take his place. They had no idea when they would be able to marry.

Lord Craven purchased a position as colonel in a regiment leaving to fight in the Caribbean and invited Tom to come along as his personal chaplain. Whatever misgivings Tom may have had about leaving his fiancée for warfare in the West Indies, he would not have turned down the request of a rich relative—especially one who held Tom's financial survival entirely in his hands. So Tom went with him. They left in early January of 1796, three years after Tom and Cassandra were engaged.

Tom was expected home in May of the following year, but instead of his anticipated homecoming, Cassandra received a letter with the news that Tom had died of yellow fever in February and been buried at sea. We can only imagine Cassandra's heartbreak at the loss of her beloved, the one she had loved but never been able to marry. There are no remaining scraps of letters that capture what she was feeling, only an observation Jane made to her cousin Eliza that Cassandra "behave[d] with a degree of resolution & Propriety which no common mind could evince in so trying a situation."[109] Cassandra seems to have been something like Elinor Dashwood, fighting her grief with the power of her mind, not allowing it supremacy.

Lord Craven said later that had he known of Tom's engagement, he wouldn't have allowed him to make the trip. The Austens, though, wouldn't have shrunk back from this kind of venture. Jane and Cassandra's brothers Frank and Charles were both in the navy and spent their lives traveling the world, at times embroiled in battle and maybe even exposed to the same yellow fever that killed Tom. Frank Austen was even in the West Indies at the same time as Tom.

Heartbreaking as that story is, what strikes me as even more sad is that beautiful Cassandra, who had just turned twenty-four when Tom died, never considered any other man. One biographer writes of the way she "hurried into spinsterly middle age."[110] Jane and Cassandra's nephew James-Edward later wrote that both sisters "were generally thought to have taken to the garb of middle age earlier than their years or their looks required."[111] It seems the harsh severity of Tom's death prompted Cassandra to close off her heart, and not only to never consider any other man, but also through her dress—her spinsterly garb—to dissuade anyone from considering her.

It's impossible to tell what Cassandra was thinking. Perhaps, like Anne Elliot with her Captain Wentworth, she knew that she loved Tom so much that she would never be able to love anyone else. Romantic as that sounds, it's horrible to think that at twenty-four Cassandra may have shut the door on love. She never lost her sense of humor, though, so it seems her life wasn't forever imbued with grief. Jane once called her "the finest comic writer of the present age,"[112] and she continued to write entertaining letters after she lost Tom. (One can imagine that if they were witty enough to entertain Jane, they would have been something.) Jane teased her about expecting a proposal from their friend James Digweed or from wealthy Sir Brook Bridges, but that was not to be. Tom Fowle would be Cassandra's only real love.

Don't feed the pain.

Jane Austen wrote in a letter to her niece Fanny, "it is no creed of mine, as you must be well aware, that such sort of Disappointments kill anybody."[113] She's speaking of heartbreak, and of the disappointment Mr. John Plumptre must have felt when Fanny made her lack of affection clear. But "such sort of Disappointment" did just about kill Marianne in *Sense and Sensibility*. The romantic Dashwood sister was determined to feel the depth of her grief when Willoughby broke her heart.

She and Willoughby had never actually been engaged, technically he had "broken no faith with [her]," but in reality he knew what he had done—he had made her believe that he loved her. He never actually said the words, but he spent hours talking to her, reading with her, singing with her or listening to her play the piano, and showed her every sort of favoritism he could. His love was "every day implied, but never professedly declared,"[114] as Marianne says.

After his abrupt departure, Marianne and Elinor go to London with Mrs. Jennings. Marianne sends Willoughby letters, jumps anxiously at every knock of the door, but still he is silent. Finally Marianne spots him across the room at an evening party. At first he ignores her, and when Marianne approaches him with affection, he hardly looks at her. He is only coldly civil. Marianne's exclamation—"Good God! Willoughby, what is the meaning of this? Have you not received my letters? Will you not shake hands with me?"[115]—does nothing to restore him to the man she knew. Willoughby quickly turns to another woman, and Marianne returns home, pale with shock, too struck even to cry.

Marianne receives one final letter from Willoughby, but it aggravates her grief rather than palliating it, and leaves her "almost scream[ing] with agony."

"I am quite at a loss to discover in what point I could be so unfortunate as to offend you," he writes. "My esteem for your whole family is very sincere; but if I have been so unfortunate as to give rise to a belief of more than I felt, or meant to express, I shall reproach myself for not having been more guarded in my professions of that esteem." Willoughby then tells Marianne that he is engaged to someone else and expects to be married within a few weeks. Elinor reads it and sees "a letter of which every line was an insult," revealing Willoughby to be "impudently cruel . . . deep in hardened villainy."[116]

Marianne, who has hardly been eating or sleeping for days, gives herself over to "unresisted grief"—a misery that she believes "nothing can do away." In a statement that proves to be prescient, Elinor urges her, "Exert yourself, dear Marianne, if you would not kill yourself."[117] But Marianne cannot—will not. She would rather attempt to "augment and fix her sorrow, by seeking silence, solitude and idleness."[118] Though she still goes out and sees people, she is entirely in her own emotional world, largely unaware of what passes around her.

Nearly three months after her disappointment with Willoughby, Marianne and Elinor leave London, heading home to their mother at Barton Cottage. They break their journey at

Cleveland Park, which is just thirty miles from Combe Magna, Willoughby's country home. On her first evening there, at twilight, Marianne walks through the shrubberies to the Grecian temple, situated on a hill. From that point, she looks out over the hills in the distance, imagining "that from their summits Combe Magna might be seen."[119]

Marianne is still cherishing these "moments of precious, invaluable misery . . . rejoic[ing] in tears of agony."[120] Her further twilight walks through wet grass leave her with a nasty cold, and with her body worn down by months of heartbreak, it grows into a more serious infection. She ends up in bed for days. Eventually she comes to a long period of "sleepless pain and delirium,"[121] which makes even Elinor believe she is not likely to live through the illness. When the danger has passed, Marianne knows that it was her feelings—her lack of self-command—that nearly killed her. "I saw that my own feelings had prepared my sufferings," she tells Elinor, "and that my want of fortitude under them had almost led me to the grave. My illness, I well knew, had been entirely brought on by myself by such negligence of my own health, as I had felt even at the time to be wrong. Had I died,—it would have been self-destruction."[122]

When there is heartbreak, there will no doubt be misery. But Austen would tell us not to "rejoice in tears of agony" or cherish the misery. Maybe she would ask as Elinor asked Marianne: "Have you no comforts? no friends?"[123] Remember those, take joy in them. Whatever you do, don't allow "such sort of Disappointments" to kill you.

Don't ignore the pain, either.

If Marianne is wrong to be so extremely romantic, so devoted to feeling everything to the fullest, whatever its consequence to her and those around her, her sister Elinor is precisely the opposite. Elinor exhibits such self-command that she barely expresses emotion at all. Here I'm not entirely sure if I'm speaking for Austen or for myself, but while Elinor's self-command is admirable, it feels excessively harsh.

When Lucy first tells Elinor of her engagement to Edward Ferrars, Austen tells us that Elinor was "almost overcome—her heart sunk within her, and she could hardly stand; but exertion was indispensably necessary; and she struggled so completely against the oppression of her feelings, that her success was speedy, and for the time complete." The reader has to be on Elinor's side here, has to rejoice that she gives Lucy Steele no opportunities to jealously gloat over her shock and disappointment. But Elinor continues to struggle against her feelings, which were "beyond any thing she had ever felt before,"[124] to subdue them, even around her mother and sister.

Elinor has reasons for this—for one, she doesn't want to distress her family. She is determined to keep her promise of secrecy to Lucy, however unworthy Lucy is of that. And she thinks that her mother's and sister's grief when they learn of Edward's engagement, will only add to her own distress, rather than be of comfort. Elinor felt that "she was stronger alone." Austen tells us, "so well was she able to answer her own expectations, that when she joined them at dinner only two hours after she had first suffered the extinction of all her dearest hopes, no one would have supposed . . . that Elinor was mourning in secret over obstacles which must divide her forever from the object of her love."[125] Only alone did she give herself "liberty to think and be wretched,"[126] but even then, she determined to keep herself busy, to talk and to act and to participate as much in normal society as possible, to do away with every appearance of brokenness and to subdue—if not eventually to eradicate—her own feelings.

Elinor continues this "unceasing exertion,"[127] this unwavering self-command, through her trip with Marianne to London, through Marianne's heartbreak with Willoughby, through visits from Edward during which Marianne makes it very clear that she still believes them to be in love. She conceals the truth until his engagement to Lucy becomes universally known. Even when finally forced to tell Marianne the news, Elinor is "far from wishing to dwell on her own feelings, or to represent herself as suffering much." Marianne is the one who cries "excessively,"[128] Elinor the one who comforts *her,* in spite of the fact that it is really Elinor's pain, not Marianne's.

Marianne is in wonder at her sister's composure. "So calm!—so cheerful!—how have you been supported?" she asks. "By feeling that I was doing my duty," Elinor replies. Always trying to make sure that no one else has to feel pain on her behalf, Elinor tells Marianne, "I would not have you suffer on my account; for I assure you I no longer suffer materially myself."[129] But clearly, as she admits to Marianne, she has been in pain—over and over through the months, as Lucy continually exulted over her. She tells Marianne:

> *If you can think me capable of ever feeling—surely you may suppose that I have suffered* now. *The composure of mind with which I have brought myself at present to consider the matter, the consolation that I have been willing to admit, have been the effect of constant and painful exertion . . . No, Marianne.—* Then, *if I had not been bound to silence, perhaps nothing could have kept me entirely—not even what I owed to my dearest friends—from openly showing that I was* very *unhappy.*[130]

As honorable as Elinor's intentions were, there's no need to "be wretched" alone. Elinor's extreme self-command is excessive, and she would have suffered less had she shared her sorrows. I may be wrong and it may be that Austen wrote with admiration of all of Elinor's emotional control. But to me the two sisters represent two extremes, one all feeling, and the other all restraint, and happiness seems to live, as in most cases, in the middle.

Show discretion.

We are probably little in need of the exhortation not to be so severe as Elinor, whose scruples did not allow her to tell even her mother and sister of her heartbreak. We're more likely to overshare, to post something on Facebook, to tweet it to the world at large and, in the midst of our emotion, to possibly send out things we later regret. No doubt Austen would encourage us to adopt at least some of Elinor's caution, to think before we parade our deepest grief in front of everyone we know and those we've "friended." I'm sure, most of all, that she would want us to be careful that in our own heartbreak we didn't malign the character of the man involved. Jane and Lizzy Bennet were cautious not to disclose Wickham's true character—and if anyone deserved some shame it was Wickham. That proves later to have been a mistake, but surely Austen would want us to err on the side of caution, especially if the guy's main character flaw is that he happened to leave us heartbroken.

Develop empathy.

Heartbreak can be so overwhelming that it blinds us to everyone else as we put all our energy into the care of our own hearts. But others around us may be walking through their own tragedies, which is another of the lessons Marianne learns. The entire time she is grieving over Willoughby, she believes her sister to be happy in Edward's love. She even chastises her, "Oh! how easy for those who have no sorrow of their own to talk of exertion! Happy, happy Elinor, *you* cannot have an idea of what I suffer."[131] Elinor, of course, is far from happy but is prevented from talking about it because of the promise she made to Lucy Steele.

When Marianne finally finds out about Elinor's own sadness, she is devastated for her and for the way she has treated her: "What!—while attending me in all my misery, has this been on your heart?—And I have reproached you for being happy!" she says. Then, after making light of Elinor's self-command, she grieves yet again for her own conduct: "Oh! Elinor, you have made me hate myself for ever.—How barbarous have I been to you!—you, who have been my only comfort, who have borne with me in all my misery, who have seemed to be only suffering for me!"[132]

No matter how great our own pain, it's worthwhile to remember that even our closest friends may be dealing with their own brokenness, even if they aren't yet ready to talk about it.

Find joy in other friends, other places.

Anne Elliot's position in *Persuasion* is not to be envied. Her father doesn't like her, because she isn't pretty enough for him to admire. Her older sister, likewise, doesn't take any interest in her or value her in the least. The mother she loved died young. Her younger sister takes advantage of Anne whenever she needs her and constantly complains. Anne's one friend in the world, Lady Russell, manages to talk her into breaking her engagement with Captain Wentworth at nineteen because he doesn't have enough money or enough standing in the world. Austen writes of Anne losing her bloom, and there's no need to wonder why.

Then Anne's heart is broken yet further. Her father, a spendthrift, has landed them in so much debt that they have to rent out the family home and live somewhere less expensive. He decides to take the family to Bath—a place Anne detests, as it's where she was sent to school just after her mother died. If it seems it can't get any worse, her father and older sister don't even want her with them in Bath, so when her younger sister Mary begs for help, Anne is sent to Uppercross to assist Mary for several months. Captain Wentworth returns to England, right in the midst of the Uppercross social circle, seeming to fall in love with Louisa, Mary's sister-in-law. He tells Mary that when he first saw Anne, he wouldn't have recognized her, she was so changed from what she used to be.

Here, of all places, Anne's bloom is restored. Mary's husband's family, the Musgroves, are kind people who genuinely like Anne—even if they're completely unaware that her heart is breaking. The Crofts, who rent the Elliot family home and are occasional guests at Uppercross, are genuinely warm and friendly. When the group decides on an impromptu trip to Lyme to visit one of Captain Wentworth's navy buddies, Anne gets to stroll to the shore in the morning and "gloried in the sea."[133] Walking back up to their hotel for breakfast, the party passes Mr. Elliot—the Elliot cousin and heir—for the first time, without knowing who he is. Austen tells us:

> *Anne's face caught his eye, and he looked at her with a degree of earnest admiration, which she could not be insensible of. She was looking remarkably well; her very regular, very pretty features, having the bloom and freshness of youth restored by the fine wind which had been blowing on her complexion, and by the animation of eye which it had also produced. It was evident that the gentleman . . . admired her exceedingly.*[134]

When Anne eventually returns to her father and sister in Bath, even her father "began to compliment her on her improved looks; he thought her 'less thin in her person, in her cheeks; her skin, her complexion, greatly improved—clearer, fresher.'"[135]

What I love about this is that Anne finds her bloom—her vibrancy—on her own, before she knows there's any hope of winning back Captain Wentworth. Wan and weary Anne Elliot becomes hale and hearty again by a change of scenery and friends. Coming from bad circumstances, from a family that didn't appreciate her, into a setting that doesn't promise to be much better, she actually finds kinship, activity, and joy. Her health and healing—emotional and physical—don't depend on any of the men in her life, though the change does wind up attracting them.

Recognize that time alone can help you know your heart.

If you've had a broken heart, then you've certainly heard that time will make it better. What Austen shows us is that time alone may give us the distance we need to really *know* our hearts. In the nine years Anne Elliot spent after first breaking her engagement to Captain Wentworth, she learned that she couldn't really love anyone else. By the end of the novel, when they are both in Bath, Anne passionately believes that whether she marries Wentworth or not, she will always love him. She realizes, "be the conclusion of the present suspense good or bad, her affection would be his for ever. Their union, she believed, could not divide her more from other men, than their final separation." Austen calls these "prett[y] musings of high-wrought love and eternal constancy"[136]—indeed.

Time gives Marianne Dashwood a much better knowledge of Willoughby's character, enough to make her realize that he never deserved her and that he could not have made her happy. Marianne learns about his lover and the way he deserted her, about his self-made financial distress. "I never could have been happy with him," she tells her mother and sister, "after knowing, as sooner or later I must have known, all this." With Elinor's guidance, she sees the selfishness that was always Willoughby's guide, even in his relationship with her. Elinor tells her:

> *The whole of his behavior . . . from the beginning to the end of the affair, has been grounded on selfishness. It was selfishness which first made him sport with your affections; which afterwards, when his own were engaged, made him delay the confession of it, and which finally carried him from Barton. His own enjoyment, or his own ease, was, in every particular, his ruling principle.*

"It is very true," Marianne replies. She now knows, "My happiness never was his object."[137]

Time gave Marianne the distance she needed to be able to see Willoughby clearly—to know that not only was her happiness never his chief aim, but also that she never would have been happy married to him. Time also helped her to see the merits of the man she never thought she would love—Colonel Brandon—the one she ended up marrying.

Time gives Elizabeth Bennet such a better perspective on Darcy's character that she begins to know that she could love him, but not until she believes it's too late, until Lydia has run off with Wickham. Just after Elizabeth confesses what's happened to Darcy, when she perceives his "gloomy" air, she begins to know: "never had she so honestly felt that she could have loved him, as now, when all love must be vain."[138]

We know that the other possible ending to the happy love Austen writes about is the misery of a broken heart. The path to love usually meanders through heartbreak—love is dangerous in that way. But in Austen's world, heartbreak leads to self-knowledge—and better knowledge of the men involved—that then in turn leads to much happier endings.

Chapter 7

Marrying Well

Jane Austen's books aren't so much about marriage, per se, as they are about the road leading to marriage and the various and inevitable pitfalls one might encounter along the way. Like so many fairy tales, Austen leads us up to the edge of happily ever after and leaves us to assume the happiness of her characters in their marital state, without spelling it out in detail. However much we may wish to know about Mr. and Mrs. Darcy's married life (and however often fan-fiction writers have taken on that project), it's not something Austen herself wanted to explore. Although, one can't help but imagine that of all things, Elizabeth and Darcy would have been happy—living in Pemberley, with Jane and Bingley not very far away, and with less desirable relatives at a much more acceptable distance.

Austen offers us glimpses of the day-to-day realities of marriage played out in the background of her novels through the lives of lesser characters. In *Pride and Prejudice,* however much Mr. Bennet tries to console himself with his books in the tranquility of his library, he's clearly unhappy in his marriage to a silly wife who feigns illness every time life upsets her. To Catherine's chagrin, Mrs. Tilney in *Northanger Abbey* was never mistreated by her husband, was not murdered by him, or shut up in the attic to live out her days in isolated desperation. But as Henry Tilney himself admits, while she lived, she may have "had much to bear"[139] because of her husband's temper and not altogether kind nature.

But not every marriage in Austen's novels is a miserable failure. My own favorite example of a good relationship is that of Admiral and Mrs. Croft in *Persuasion*. The pair met and married so quickly that they measure the length of their courtship in days rather than weeks or months and are ashamed to admit its actual duration to Anne. In spite of the disaster one might expect from a quick—if not hasty—marriage, they can't stand to be apart from each other. Mrs. Croft has spent much of their fifteen married years on board ship with her husband, crossing the Atlantic, traveling to places as distant as the East Indies on one end and Bermuda on the other. She explains:

> *While we were together, you know, there was nothing to be feared. . . . The only time that I ever really suffered in body or mind, the only time that I ever fancied myself unwell, or had any ideas of danger, was the winter that I passed by myself at Deal, when the Admiral (Captain Croft then) was in the North Seas. I lived in perpetual fright at that time, and had all manner of imaginary complaints from not knowing what to do with myself, or when I should hear from him next; but as long as we could be together, nothing ever ailed me . . .*[140]

Austen leaves us in no doubt that the Admiral feels the same way about his wife. I love that after all those years the Crofts still find themselves essential to each other's happiness.

Two things drastically separate marriage in Austen's day from our own. First, marriage was a permanent state. Aside from extremely rare cases of divorce (as we see with the Rushworths in *Mansfield Park*), there was no getting out of it. Today we still say those vows and no doubt when we say them have the best of "til death do us part" intentions, but we also know that marriage can be gotten out of if necessary. Divorce is almost always horribly painful and messy, but it provides a fail-safe if the vows become unworkable, if they are broken beyond repair, or if the marriage simply no longer makes us happy. We know that and even in the midst of our vow-taking, we can't *un*-know it. There will always be an out. That is both a bane and a luxury for modern-day couples—one that was not available to Austen's characters and contemporaries.

The second radical distinction is that marriage was often a necessity. A lady would never have worked in Austen's day. If she were quite desperate, and at the lowest end of the social scale, she might have become a governess, or a lady's companion, but those would have been her sole options, and only pursued in cases of absolute necessity. The only real acceptable path for a woman was marriage; it was her source of income and security. If she had little money, it would have been essential for her to marry as well as possible to ensure her own survival and that of her family. If she had much money, it still would have been imperative for her to marry well, to preserve and increase her family's social standing. We have the luxury today of pursuing whatever career we choose, of having a million different means of paying the bills and putting food on the table—and we are actually responsible for ourselves, rather than being forever dependent on our families. Marriage is an option *if* we want it (and most of us do), not something we are forced into in order to preserve our dignity.

Despite those differences Austen knew what made a good marriage, then and now. She understood what it meant to marry well—and how much more that encompassed than mere money. Even with her comparatively scant writing on the realities of married life, she still has excellent advice.

Whatever you do, don't marry without love.

Women in Austen's era would have needed this guidance more than we do. They would have been tempted to marry for money alone—or, less crassly, just to ensure that they would always have a place to live and food on the table. We wouldn't think of marrying for any reason other than for love. (Would we?) As Jane Bennet says, "Oh, Lizzy! do any thing rather than marry without affection."[141] In one of Austen's wonderful letters to her niece Fanny, she tells her, "nothing can be compared to the misery of being bound *without* Love, bound to one, & preferring another. *That* is a Punishment which you do *not* deserve."[142]

I think of Charlotte Lucas in *Pride and Prejudice,* marrying the obsequious, ridiculous Mr. Collins. When Lizzy refuses him, Charlotte determines to have him for herself, "solely from the pure and disinterested desire of an establishment"[143]—determinedly blind to his faults and willing to put up with them to have the comfortable living at Rosings, with the grand patroness Lady Catherine de Bourgh. Blind as Charlotte attempts to be, and though she is engaged to Mr. Collins after only having known him a very short while, she had to be aware of "the stupidity with which he was favoured by nature."[144] Yet as a twenty-seven-year-old woman with little money and who had never been good looking, marriage to Mr. Collins was Charlotte's "preservative from want."[145] However painful, a marriage to Mr. Collins was her security.

Austen knew what it was to contemplate marrying without love, but she couldn't go through with it. When she was just about to turn twenty-seven—an age at which the prospect of marriage became less and less likely—a neighbor and friend proposed. Harris Bigg-Wither was the younger brother of Jane and Cassandra's dear friends, Elizabeth, Catherine, and Alethea Bigg. He stammered and had been sickly as a child, but he was sensible, tall, and set to inherit a large estate not far from where the Austens grew up in the village of Steventon. Jane and Cassandra went to stay with the family for a few weeks, and seven days into the trip, Harris proposed. We only know that Jane accepted him that evening and then withdrew her acceptance in the morning, after which she and Cassandra quickly left the house and went back to join their parents in Bath, cutting their visit short. We can only imagine what that night must have been like for Jane, awake and wondering what to do, eventually realizing that she never should have accepted Harris's proposal and having to withdraw her consent.

Austen's niece Caroline wrote about the affair later, saying of Harris, "a great many would have taken him *without* love." His estate, his position in the world, was enough that most women during that time would have married him anyway. But that would not do for Jane. She couldn't marry someone she didn't love, no matter how advantageous the match, no matter how much better off she would have been financially, or how much security it could have given her family—especially her mother and sister. Austen's niece continues, "I beleive [*sic*] most young women so circumstanced would have taken Mr. W. & trusted to love after marriage."[146] Jane Austen, however, could not. Austen showed her great courage here. She couldn't do what *most* would have done, she couldn't do what many would have expected her to do, she had to follow her heart.

DON'T LEAVE YOUR HAPPINESS TO CHANCE.

Early in *Pride and Prejudice,* Charlotte Lucas explains her views on marriage to Lizzy: "Happiness in marriage is entirely a matter of chance," she says. (Or, as a boyfriend told me once, "It's a complete crap shoot." So romantic.) No matter how much two people are alike, Charlotte explains, after they marry they will change anyway and become different enough to get on each other's nerves. She concludes, "It is better to know as little as possible of the defects of the person with whom you are to pass your life."[147] Austen would never condone that sort of blind leap into marriage, nor the underlying crap-shoot philosophy.

If Charlotte was determinedly blind and thought there was no point in knowing her future spouse, our own focus on our feelings may leave us in the dark as well. We get caught up in the gushy-ness of romance, the twitterpations, the falling-in-love butterflies. Our emotions are paramount, and the guy who makes us feel the best is clearly the one we should marry.

Austen wouldn't condone this approach any more than Charlotte's blind leap. For her, deciding to marry wasn't about *feeling* it was right, but *knowing* it was right. Of course, there's romance involved, but marriage wasn't just about mushy feelings, it was serious business and required serious thought—something we may miss in her stories if we don't read them carefully. A woman in Austen's day couldn't afford *not* to think carefully about who she married. She couldn't get out of the marriage, and she would have very little life outside her home and family. So much of her future happiness (or despair) was dependent on the man she chose; she couldn't trust her decision only to the whims of her feelings.

On the road to marriage, Austen's characters *love,* but they also *think*—mainly about their suitor's character and how acceptable or unacceptable his manners and morals are. It may not sound sexy, but it assured them—as much as possible—of years of happiness later.

Believe that marriage can be life-affirming and joyful—even as a permanent state.

I think this is Austen's main message to us about marriage, and one we crave in our divorce-ridden era. Although Austen never married herself, she knew about the happiness of marriage by proxy, by watching her parents and brothers. She soaked up everything she knew about the happiness of married life from those closest to her.

Jane's parents—George and Cassandra—seem to have been very happy. Although our knowledge is certainly limited, there's no evidence of affairs on the side, nothing pointing to great friction. They met most likely in Oxford, where George was a scholar at St. John's College and Cassandra was probably visiting her uncle. With only the income from George's country parish, along with small inheritances, they would have anticipated a life of hard work. But they were eager and ready. They went on to have eight children (never adopting the only readily available birth control of separate bedrooms) and their house seems to have been full of laughter and love.

Cassandra wrote witty little poems to commemorate family events or just for fun; the family read together in the evenings. The children played and put on plays in the barn for family and friends—no doubt with the encouragement of their parents. George had grown up as an orphan and for that reason may have prized his family more, understanding through his own want as a child the true value of family. He loved his wife and didn't want to travel without her, and she didn't want to travel without her children. The family never had a great deal of money, but they seem to have had an abundance of happiness and love. No family is perfect, and the Austens certainly weren't. When Jane's sister Cassandra destroyed Jane's letters, she no doubt took out anything that would have revealed deep conflict. While the children were close, even in the remaining letters and passed down family history, you get a sense of some bristling and offenses—individuals who could be demanding, some who liked one better than the other.

Overall though, I think it's fair to say that the Austens were happy, and that when Jane wrote about the Darcys and Bingleys, with their great hope of marital happiness, she based that happiness and joy to some degree on the marriage closest to her: her parents. By the time George died, the Austens had been married forty years.

As the next-to-youngest in a family of eight children, Jane also grew up watching her brothers marry and establish their families. Five of the six Austen sons married (all except for the second, George, who appears to have been mentally deficient in some way), and they were largely happy. None of them seem to have married for money; while they married prudently, all of them married for love. That fact no doubt impressed Jane, living in an era with so many other lesser reasons to marry.

One of the most poignant stories of the Austen brothers' loving marriages is that of Edward. As a child Edward had actually been chosen by wealthy cousins to inherit their estates; the

Knights couldn't have children of their own and fell in love with Edward when they came through Steventon on their wedding tour. So Edward eventually adopted the last name of Knight and was elevated into a world of wealth and privilege. At twenty-four, he fell in love with Elizabeth Bridges, a "graceful, brown-haired beaut[y]"[148] and daughter of a wealthy family. Because money was no issue, they were married relatively quickly, when Elizabeth was just eighteen.

At thirty-five years old, after seventeen years of marriage, Elizabeth delivered her eleventh baby. To all appearances, baby and mother were fine. Two weeks later, Elizabeth died suddenly half an hour after dinner. The reason for Elizabeth's death was never known. The whole Austen family was thrown into shock and grief. Letters between Jane and Cassandra—who was staying with Edward's family to help with the new baby—chronicle their great sadness.

Jane writes of her brother, "dearest Edward," and of his sufferings. She knows that his "loss is terrible, & must be felt as such." Edward's grief must have been great for a time. Jane writes, "these are too early days indeed to think of Moderation in greif [*sic*]." She imagines "poor Edward restless in Misery going from one room to the other—& perhaps not seldom upstairs to see all that remains of his Elizabeth."[149]

This is not the grief of a man who didn't love his wife, or who only viewed her in light of her monetary value, but rather that of one who was deeply in love and irreparably wounded by losing her. Edward was forty-two when Elizabeth died. In his position, with his wealth, he certainly could have married again easily, yet he never did. There are many possible reasons for this, but I think it's probable he simply never met anyone he could have loved the way he loved "his Elizabeth."

In the Austen family—as in Austen's books—marriages were made for love, were joyful, even as a permanent state, and were something to be greatly mourned when they were lost too early.

Don't expect perfect happiness.

As much as we may be tempted to think so, the picture Austen gives us of marriage isn't the saccharine happily-ever-after of fairy tales. She writes of eighteen-year-old Catherine Morland in *Northanger Abbey* beginning "perfect happiness"[150] with her marriage to Henry Tilney (and who wouldn't have been perfectly happy with witty and kind Henry Tilney?), but I suspect this effusion of enthusiasm for marriage on Austen's part is in keeping with the generally sarcastic tone of the novel. Throughout the book Austen writes tongue-in-cheek about the then-accepted idea of heroines, using Catherine to turn that notion on its head. Catherine is hardly "an heroine"[151] as Austen describes her. She will no doubt have a contentedly happy marriage, though not the idealized perfection every heroine (of fairy tales or gothic romances, as the case may be) receives.

Austen tells us a lot about the happiness of her couples. Anne "was tenderness itself"[152] for her Captain Wentworth, and he loved her back in equal measure. Colonel Brandon had consolation in Marianne "for every past affliction," and "Marianne found her own happiness in forming his."[153] Austen writes of the "perfect happiness of the union" between Emma and Mr. Knightley. And although the "married cousins" of *Mansfield Park* may make us cringe a bit, Austen credits them with "true love," and with a "home of affection and comfort."[154]

But Austen isn't really interested in calm, blissful (dare I say bland) marital perfection. About fictional characters, she says, "Pictures of perfection as you know make me sick & wicked."[155] She's interested in real, good marriages between real people, with all their faults and foibles—and her characters have plenty of those.

In a wonderful scene between Admiral and Mrs. Croft in *Persuasion,* we see the Admiral struggling to keep their carriage from turning over as he drives them around the English countryside. He may be quite adept at sea, but on land he needs his wife to occasionally commandeer the reins and ensure they don't hit posts or dung-carts. Anne imagines this to be "no bad representation of the general guidance of their affairs,"[156] and we can assume she's right. Austen tells us that Mrs. Croft was better at handling their business affairs as well. The picture that emerges is that of a wife needing to cover for her husband, who, however much loved, can be somewhat inept at the things that a man perhaps *should* be good at.

In *Pride and Prejudice,* Austen writes of Darcy's sister Georgiana being alarmed at the "lively, sportive, manner"[157] that Elizabeth uses with Darcy after they are married—no different than the lively manner she used with him before their marriage, no doubt. You can see Elizabeth giving Darcy a hard time, playfully poking fun at him and drawing him out of his somewhat stuffy, proud self. But this assumes that Darcy had faults at which to poke fun. Even with all the things Darcy and Elizabeth learned *en route* to marriage, with all the progress they made perfecting their own characters, it's not difficult to imagine that they may each have struggled with imperfections afterward—both in themselves and each other.

No, Austen leaves us in no doubt of her characters' great imperfection before their marriages, and, while they are improved by their journeys through the course of the novels, we can hardly think they are perfect at the end. And as such, their marriages—though undoubtedly happy—cannot be quite perfect, either.

Cultivate the ability to take—and give—correction.

We've talked about this before because it's at the heart of Austen's stories. So many of her characters make grave errors or have deep character flaws that need to be excised. And so many of them come face to face with their faults when they're confronted by their would-be suitors, whether it's the kind-but-firm correction of Emma's Mr. Knightley, or the outraged accusations between Lizzy and Darcy.

It is the most difficult of Austen's lessons to swallow, and perhaps the most foreign to our own era. It reminds me of when I was a child and my mother, trying to correct me about something, would tell me that I needed to have "a teachable spirit." I didn't want a teachable spirit. I wanted to be right, and I wanted to be left alone. In Austen's day, gentlemen and ladies—not all of them, surely, but those Austen cherishes—made it a priority to ferret out their own flaws, to rightly know themselves and ensure that they could withstand scrutiny. We are less anxious to know our own faults, quicker to take offense. But for a long and happy marriage, Austen would have us develop these talents.

Of course, these scenes in Austen's novels often come with fireworks, and that's realistic. She would probably have us try to avoid a Darcy-and-Elizabeth-style face-off and aim for something gentler. There is bound to be conflict in any marriage, though, and it's bound to be related to something one or the other of us has done. Being able to talk through those things, to withstand and perhaps eventually even welcome correction, bodes well for enduring happiness, even if the price is temporary discomfort.

Cherish your "respect, esteem, and confidence" in your spouse.

When we think of the things that make a marriage work, of course we think about faithfulness, and probably after that a sense of humor and a good sex life. Austen would wholeheartedly agree—at least and especially about the sense of humor—but would ultimately tie long-term happiness to more solid things. The story she gives us of Mr. Bennet in *Pride and Prejudice* is telling. He married his wife because he was "captivated by youth and beauty, and that appearance of good humour, which youth and beauty generally give." Too late, Mr. Bennet learned that his wife had few thoughts in her idle, foolish head. Her "weak understanding . . . had very early in their marriage put an end to all real affection for her." Jane Austen, champion of women's cognitive abilities, cannot allow a sensible man to be happy with a thoughtless wife. She concludes: "Respect, esteem, and confidence, had vanished for ever; and all his views of domestic happiness were overthrown."[158]

Where we may worry foremost about the death of romance, Austen is chiefly concerned about the death of respect—not because romance is unimportant to her, but because to Austen the one is impossible without the other. Where there were no thoughtful discussions, or at least reasonable conversations, where there was no esteem, Austen held out little hope for the "domestic happiness" of the couple concerned. Mr. Bennet finds one source of pleasure in laughing at his wife's "ignorance and folly,"[159] but it's not a pleasure Austen envies.

I think if we sensed romance fading in a long-term relationship, Austen would encourage us to look at its foundation, to remember the solid things on which it is built. We may be tempted to throw out a relationship that doesn't live up to our own overly romantic notions, but Austen would remind us that ephemeral romance grows out of these more staid (if somewhat boring) things. Romantic feelings may be whimsical and unpredictable, but when you are sure of your husband's worth, when you respect his understanding and feel confident of his character, affection will always be there, along with the potential for happiness.

Be thankful that you can choose to be single.

For those of us who are single and pining for marriage, there is a name that may offer us some relief: Charlotte Collins. It's always helpful to remember that there are worse things than being single—like being married to someone as ridiculous as Mr. Collins. Much as Charlotte may have preferred to go into marriage knowing as little about her partner as possible, Austen tells us that she knew that he "was neither sensible nor agreeable; his society was irksome, and his attachment to her must be imaginary."[160] Once married, she blushes at her husband's contrived, fawning speeches. She encourages him to work in his garden, no doubt so she can be alone in the house. But she is unable to entirely neglect all the duties of a wife, and soon is expecting a child. It's horrible to think of, from our secure spot two centuries later.

Thankfully, we don't have the same societal pressures forcing us into a marriage like that. How much Charlotte would envy us our freedom.

For Austen, a well-made marriage—one carefully built and considered—could be beautiful and loving, could fulfill those "til death" vows until death brought heartbreak with it. Those are the kinds of marriages she would want for us.

Chapter 8

Cherishing Family and Friends

Jane Austen lived with her family for her entire life. Unlike today, where families scatter across the globe, Jane was tied to her family and couldn't have escaped them had she wanted to. Single women then rarely lived on their own—except perhaps in cases like Austen's Emma, who, had she not married Mr. Knightley, would have been well established, wealthy enough to be self-sufficient. There was no fortune for Austen herself to inherit, which left her living with her parents into her adult years. Thankfully, she loved her family and was content to have them form the largest part of her social circle.

Growing up in a house full of boys, with six brothers and one sister, along with Mr. Austen's pupils, Jane was surrounded by joyful chaos. Her confidant and closest friend was always her sister Cassandra, three years older—"the girls," as they were known in the family. The boys grew and went their ways: James studied at Oxford and became ordained; Edward inherited and managed the estates of wealthy relatives; Henry eventually went into banking, and later the church; Frank and Charles went very young to the naval academy and had swashbuckling careers on the seas, fighting the French and the rest of Britain's enemies. The two girls continued to live with their parents, first in the little village they grew up in, then in Bath after their father retired. Their lives revolved around visits to and from family—mostly their brothers and their brothers' many children.

Austen's letters overflow with family love. Most of them are from Jane to Cassandra, and find the sisters lamenting being apart for long periods of time, usually when one went to visit a brother's family. Jane signs off to Cassandra in one letter, sending her "Infinities of Love."[161] In another she charges her, "Take care of your precious self, do not work too hard."[162] They shared with each other all the details—the "important nothings"[163]—of their lives. If anyone knew everything about Jane, it was Cassandra. When Jane died, Cassandra wrote:

> *I* have *lost a treasure, such a Sister, such a friend as never can have been surpassed,—She was the sun of my life, the gilder of every pleasure, the soother of every sorrow, I had not a thought concealed from her, & it is as if I had lost a part of myself.*[164]

No doubt Cassandra played the same role for Jane—as "soother of every sorrow," from whom nothing was concealed. It's fair to say that Jane would never have been the Jane Austen we know and love without her sister.

The letters also show the girls sewing shirts for their many brothers, commenting on their growing nieces and nephews, joking with each other and within the family about who they might or might not marry—along with such details of daily life like the design of a henhouse or the price of beef. They hope for and rejoice in promotions for Frank and Charles in their naval careers, wondering how soon they will see them back on land. Jane chastises Charles for using his naval prize money to buy her and Cassandra topaz crosses. She writes of her "rambles" by the sea with brother Henry, who she says "cannot help being amusing."[165] ("Oh! What a Henry,"[166] she writes.) Of tenderhearted Edward, Jane wrote that she knew "no one more deserving of happiness without alloy."[167] The letters track Jane going to spend time with Henry in London, staying at Edward's large country house, and living with Frank and his wife in Southampton after Mr. Austen died. When Jane and Cassandra were home for longer periods, they often had a niece or a nephew come to stay for weeks at a time, to be loved and entertained by their aunts.

Jane also reports regularly to Cassandra on Mrs. Austen's recurring health problems, but the tone is one of concern rather than annoyance. Unlike Mrs. Bennet in *Pride and Prejudice,* Mrs. Austen's spirits were "as good as ever," and her "maladies" were not "often thought of."[168] Alas, Mr. Austen would be the first to die, and Jane had to write to her brother Frank to break the news. She writes, "His tenderness as a Father, who can do justice to?" The family clearly knew they were loved by their father, as "Objects so beloved, so fondly cherished as his wife and Children ever were."[169] The Austen family love was one that reached down to the next generation's many grandchildren, nieces, and nephews. Mrs. Austen writes to her granddaughter Anna, "indeed, my dear Anna, there is nobody I think of oftener, very few I love better."[170] And that generation clearly reciprocated. A young Louisa, Edward's daughter, borrowed a little part of one of Jane's letters to send her Aunt Cassandra "a Hundred Thousand Million Kisses."[171] The letters and these sweet little phrases are tender remnants of a loving family.

Love your family (in spite of their imperfections).

If you are feeling overwhelmed—surely no family could compete with the Austens and all that love—it helps to know that they weren't at all perfect. Cassandra often spent months with Edward's family at their house in Kent, helping out with their eleven children, but Jane was less in demand there. It seems Jane's sharp wit may have been a bit too much for Edward's sweet wife. Jane loved those eleven children, but she admitted that they could be a handful. She wrote of one of their governesses, "I pity her, tho' they *are* my nieces."[172] And as Edward's children grew, Jane wrote critically of the older boys, for their love of luxury and hunting and neglect of more important things. Cassandra destroyed the letter with Jane's criticism, so we only see the remaining wafts of negativity in subsequent correspondence.

Her eldest brother James and his wife Mary were a source of greater conflict. For a period after Mr. Austen's death, Jane, Cassandra, and their mother lived with their brother Frank and his family in Southampton. Expecting a visit from James, Jane wrote:

> *I am sorry & angry that his Visits should not give one more pleasure; the company of so good & so clever a Man ought to be gratifying in itself;—but his Chat seems all forced, his Opinions on many points too much copied from his Wife's, & his time here is spent I think in walking about the House & banging the Doors, or ringing the Bell for a glass of Water.*[173]

It's one of the few critical moments in Jane's letters that doesn't feel infused with wit and humor, and the picture it creates of James is that of a demanding and ill-at-ease guest. It makes me wish even more to read all those letters Cassandra destroyed. But after spending an extended period of time with family, most of us can relate to the little and sometimes larger frustrations.

Family recollections of James's wife Mary show her to be insecure and difficult, subject to petty jealousies even with other members of the family. She was James's second wife, and never gave Anna, his daughter from his first marriage, quite the love she needed. (Unfortunately, James neglected Anna as well, in favor of his two younger children—which must have made her grandmother and aunts' love that much more precious to the growing girl.) Jane writes of Mary, though it's unclear exactly what she's referring to, "How can Mrs J. Austen be so provokingly ill-judging?—I should have expected better from her. . . . "[174] What probably made her more difficult for Jane to love was that she was no great reader. Writing about a book the family was reading together in the evening, one she found delightfully amusing, Jane says, "Mary, I believe, has little pleasure from that or any other book."[175] That would be high condemnation from Jane Austen.

Then there were more distant relatives also providing challenges. Wealthy Aunt Leigh-Perrot could be vexing—but then, wealthy relatives were put up with, irritating or not. Cousin Edward Cooper was a clergyman with a strong evangelical bent, and while Jane didn't entirely oppose the evangelical and more conservative branch of the church, she didn't appreciate Edward's particular interpretation nor the "Letters of cruel comfort"[176] he was known to send at especially challenging times. When invited to visit the Coopers, the Austens were likely to find convenient commitments elsewhere, like a visit to the coast. Jane writes, "for the present we greatly prefer the sea to all our relations."[177]

If the Austens were a loving family, they were also a normal family with the difficulties and annoyances that entails.

Jane wrote about several far from ideal and at times horrible families—*Pride and Prejudice*'s ill-matched Bennets with their apathetic child-rearing; the cold, unloving Elliots of *Persuasion;* grasping Mr. Tilney in *Northanger Abbey.* It's possible that there were hints of these faults in her own family, that her imagination worked on the realities she saw around her to picture what they might have become had there not been any restraint.

But the Austens were not horrible, they were just normal. And they continued to love each other. Sometimes onerous brother James would be welcomed for each visit, along with his non-book-loving wife. Jane sincerely mourned Edward's wife Elizabeth when she died, even if Jane was aware that she was not Elizabeth's favorite. No doubt there were a multitude of other little vexations, but at the heart of the Austen family was a great deal of love that held them together in spite of all of that.

Be there.

One evidence of the Austens' tight bond is the way they simply were there for each other. When Edward's wife Elizabeth died, Cassandra was staying with the family to help with the new baby. She extended her visit for four months, so she could be there to comfort and assist with running the household until fifteen-year-old Fanny could step into that role. No doubt that would have been a daunting task for Fanny, with ten younger brothers and sisters, reeling from the grief of having just lost her mother. Jane writes to Cassandra, "You will be everything to [Fanny], you will give her all the Consolation that human aid can give."[178] Brother Henry drove down immediately from London to be with Edward. Frank came a month later, when he was back on land and could get leave. James and his wife Mary collected Edward's eldest boys from their school at Winchester and kept them for a week, until they went to stay with their grandmother and Aunt Jane, who took great joy not only in talking to them about "the most serious of all concerns,"[179] but entertaining them with all kinds of games—"paper ships, riddles, conundrums, and cards"[180]—and taking them rowing on the river, looking at the naval ships, and generally keeping them happily busy.

You see the same concern when Henry became dangerously ill. Jane had been visiting Henry in London, working on the negotiations and details of getting *Emma* published, when what seemed like a simple illness in Henry suddenly became life-threatening. Jane immediately wrote to bring her brothers and sister to London. Charles was at sea and Frank's wife was about to give birth, but Edward, James, and Cassandra came immediately and stayed until Henry was out of danger. Again, when Mr. Austen died, Mrs. Austen and the girls were left in some financial need, so the brothers contributed what they could from their own incomes. Frank set up house with them, and eventually Edward gave them a cottage on his estate at Chawton. Whatever an Austen faced, they did not face it alone.

In *Pride and Prejudice* when Lydia runs off with Wickham, her immediate family is largely unable to help. Her father has no resources to hunt Wickham down and her mother is reduced to sitting upstairs in her room having fainting fits. Lydia's aunt and uncle Gardiner step in. They are competent, coolheaded, and determined. They put up with Lydia in spite of her terribly ungrateful spirit and see that she is quickly and honorably married. Darcy, of course, has done much of the work and paid all the bills, and they end up in large part simply taking credit in his place, but without them the family would have been lost. Jane Austen had family like the Gardiners—the kind who step in and take care of you, who are reliable and steady.

Make an effort.

Perhaps we're more ready to be there for our family in times of need than we are to just be there for no particular reason. In Austen's era, and with her family, visits were an unquestioned and (mostly) welcomed matter of course that sometimes lasted months. Of course that's not practical now. We only get two weeks off and may live thousands of miles apart. We don't have a great house in the country where we can all fit comfortably, with governesses to help watch the children. But it bears remembering that you can't really be close to people you don't spend time with.

When the Austen family was separated, long letters were regularly sent back and forth. Again, we hardly have time for writing out weekly missives in longhand, but how much easier it is with e-mail, cell phones, and Skype. We can be part of each other's lives from wherever we happen to have Wi-Fi.

Forget about sibling rivalry.

Reading Jane's letters you can't help but be struck by how much the Austen brothers and sisters simply cheered each other on. Maybe they were in an ideal situation for sibling generosity: None of the rest had dreams of being novelists, so they weren't threatened by Jane's success. Because neither Jane nor Cassandra married, there could be no contention over whose husband had more money or a better place in society. For the most part, the brothers went in different directions, so they wouldn't have directly competed. Even where they were in the same field—like Frank and Charles, both in the navy—they seem to have helped each other along rather than lording their successes over each other.

The siblings desperately wanted Frank and Charles to receive promotions and succeed in their naval careers and worried about them when there was threat of harm. (Jane even borrowed the names of Frank's ships and used them in *Mansfield Park.*) Their hearts broke for Henry when he went bankrupt. Henry himself was so proud of Jane that he had to tell his friends that she was the author of *Pride and Prejudice* and *Sense and Sensibility.* She had no desire to be known as the author, but her bursting older brother couldn't keep her secret. Even Cassandra, who could have resented Jane for shirking some of the household duties in order to write, felt nothing but joy and pride. After Jane died, Cassandra wrote in the margin of her copy of *Persuasion,* "Dear dear Jane! This deserves to be written in letters of gold."[181] Perhaps it wasn't always entirely easy, in a family where one brother was singled out to inherit the estates of relatives and thus become rich. In one letter to Cassandra, Jane writes, "I am tolerably glad to hear that Edward's income is so good a one—as glad as I can at anybody's being rich besides You & me."[182] But when that rich brother was tenderhearted, kind, and generous, his wealth was easier to bear.

Know that your "unfortunate relations" don't have to define you.

Jane Austen knew that wonderful daughters sometimes end up with unfortunate fathers and mothers. One of her recurring themes is that no matter the faults of your family of origin, they don't have to define you. We see this so clearly in *Pride and Prejudice* with Jane and Elizabeth Bennet. Their mother is foolish and thoughtless. Their father is thoughtful but not entirely loving. His great joy is a good laugh, and finding many reasons to laugh at his wife, he doesn't hesitate to do so in front of his own children. Instead of using his talents to shape his children, he becomes indolent, retreats to his library, and allows them to become what they will. The result is foolish Kitty and Lydia, following entirely in their mother's footsteps, and pedantic, joyless Mary, who strives to be known as being accomplished for her little talent. The older girls, Lizzy and Jane, are stunning examples of good sense, kindness, and decorum. Little that they inherited and little that they were taught, they made the most of it; at some point determining to be different. Who of us hasn't at one point thought that we would never in a million years be like our mother? Jane and Lizzy had every reason to strive for that goal, and in spite of every odd against them, they entirely succeeded.

In *Persuasion,* lovely Anne is the only Elliot worth knowing, however much her father prides himself on his place in society. He cared for his daughters based only on how he esteemed their beauty and how well he thought they would marry. He didn't care for family so much as he cared for connections. Anne's older sister Elizabeth is cruel and doesn't value her—she is "only Anne"[183] after all. Younger Mary is hardly kind and carries on the family tradition of thinking chiefly of herself—how she has been offended, how people ought to be treating her, how ill she is. Somehow in the midst of all of that, Anne becomes patient, thoughtful, and kind. She inherited her mother's gentle spirit. When we meet her at twenty-seven, she is painfully aware of her own family's failings.

In a world where single women were dependent on their families, Austen recognized that not everyone was as fortunate as she was. She celebrated those who were circumspect, who had enough self-knowledge to judge their own families fairly and see their disastrous weaknesses. Austen understood the strength it took to determine to be something different with no encouragement from those closest to you. She would want us to understand the same, and to know that whatever the failings we grew up with, we don't need to carry them with us—that families provide our beginning but not necessarily our definition.

Cherish your true friends.

Jane Austen was not gregarious. She never wanted to have hordes of friends. If she lived today, she would never participate in something like Twitter or Facebook (or whatever will be the next big thing). She's actually reported to have been shy. In one of my favorite quotes, she says, "I do not want People to be very agreable [*sic*], as it saves me the trouble of liking them a great deal."[184] Later in life, anticipating a carriage ride with acquaintances, she writes, "It is uphill work to be talking to those whom one knows so little."[185] She didn't want to be surrounded by a crowd. She never needed to be popular. She wanted to be quiet and happy with the few people who were dear to her.

Austen kept a handful of friendships for nearly her whole life. Martha Lloyd moved into the neighborhood when Jane was thirteen, and although she was ten years Jane's senior, she quickly became close to both Jane and Cassandra. (Her sister Mary would later become brother James Austen's somewhat difficult wife.) Elegant Martha was a "desperate Walker"[186] like Jane and joined her on her treks around the countryside. Jane writes of staying with her after a ball, of the two of them wide awake until two in the morning talking—no doubt about the men they had danced with, the men they wished they had danced with, and what everyone wore.

The Bigg sisters—Elizabeth, Catherine, and Alethea—moved into the neighborhood at roughly the same time. All around the same age as Jane and Cassandra, the five girls would stay close for the rest of their lives. Jane and Cassandra paid regular visits to the Bigg estate at Manydown, and it was at a ball there, actually, that Jane danced with Tom Lefroy. In spite of the awkwardness that happened with their younger brother Harris—whose proposal to Jane was first accepted then rejected the following morning—the friendships remained steady. It says something about the strength of the connection and the determination of all the girls that not even that kind of discord could create a rupture.

Another in Jane's close circle was Anne Sharp, who Jane didn't meet until she was nearly thirty when Anne was governess to Jane's brother Edward's children. Throughout her life Anne would struggle with her health and employment, but Jane hoped for better things for her "excellent kind friend."[187] Eventually Anne went to work as governess for widowed Lady Pilkington, and Jane hoped more than anything that Lady Pilkington's single brother-in-law William—who inherited the baronetcy of her deceased husband—would love her friend Anne. "I do so want him to marry her!" she writes. "Oh! Sir Wm—Sir Wm—how I will love you, if you will love Miss Sharp!"[188] (Alas, that was not to be.)

Jane had opportunities to meet many others but was more likely to comment on their faults than to determine to like them. Perhaps if we had more of her letters, we would know of other close friendships, but it seems like this small group, along with some intimates among her extended family connections, were all she really wanted. She would hope the best for them, laugh with them (no doubt a great deal), grieve with them, and long for their visits. If she had few friends, she made up for it with the depth of those relationships. It's a pattern that repeats itself in her books as well: Characters tend to have one or two close friends, like Elizabeth Bennet with Charlotte Lucas (at least until Charlotte becomes Mrs. Collins), or Anne Elliot with Lady Russell and Mrs. Smith. Sisters are precious in Austen's stories as well, the way Cassandra was in her own life. It's fair to say that Jane and Lizzy Bennet could not have survived without each other.

Today we often value ourselves by the number of people we know, by the hundreds or thousands following us online. Austen would advise us to cherish our small circle of dear ones and not worry so much about the rest.

Know that friends can become family.

Jane and Cassandra's dear friend Martha Lloyd lost her mother in 1805, leaving her fairly alone in the world and basically homeless. Without seeming to think twice about it, the Austens welcomed Martha into their own family. Since Mr. Austen had recently passed away, the Austen household then consisted of Mrs. Austen, Jane, Cassandra, and Martha. Martha would stay with the family until she left to become Frank's second wife at the late age of sixty-three. In their early years as friends, Jane wrote to Cassandra about planning to have the three of them together under the same roof, "Who will be so happy as we?"[189] Martha continued to be dear, becoming "the friend and Sister under every circumstance."[190]

Jane and Cassandra had plenty of family of their own, but their hearts and home were open to their dear friend. There was no question of Martha being left to shift for herself, always going from one relative to the next in order to not wear out her welcome. She had a constant in the Austens—a place she belonged, where she would always be embraced. For those of us whose families are not around, or perhaps like the Elliots simply incapable of loving, no doubt Jane would wish the same. She would want family to spring up for us from other sources, knowing it might be even more precious because it wasn't technically our own.

Jane Austen adored her family and her small group of friends. Where cherishing were possible, she would advise us to cherish those closest to us—both family and friends—to build into their lives, to be present, to value them more than hundreds of "friends" or "followers." She would want us to hold on to our dear ones. She would have faith, too, that if our family beginnings were unenviable, they need not limit what we can become or who we can be.

Chapter 9

Saving and Spending

It's one of the great injustices of the world that Jane Austen made little money on her writing, when others have made millions adapting and playing off of her work. Had she gotten what she deserved, she would have been wealthy—she would have had the tens of thousands of pounds a year she gave to her wealthy heroes. As it was, she made less than £700 during her lifetime, and it seems that she sensibly invested most of that, rather than enjoying it.

Austen delighted in wealth and the "Elegance & Ease & Luxury"[191] it could buy. But she didn't grow up with wealth, and most of her life was spent anxiously maintaining a careful sufficiency. When the Austen family was young, Jane's father George had difficulty keeping the ends together, as it were; with children coming one after the other he was continually scraping by. He worked very hard and still had to borrow from relatives. By the time Jane was in her teens, her parents were more secure, but money was never something that flowed in the Austen home. As unfair as it is, Jane never had an abundance.

Recognize that money is essential, but not essential to happiness.

Growing up in such an environment, I believe Austen learned two lessons about money that she carried with her the rest of her life. The first was that money is essential. Austen would have been conscious of the lower edges of society, of those who didn't have wealthy relatives to help when help was needed. In a world where government welfare was nonexistent, where a lady would rarely if ever actually earn anything, one of life's ongoing themes was dependence. It mattered how much your father owned, what he inherited, what he would be able to give you, whether your mother's wealthy brother would include you in his will. And all of those things were entirely out of your control. After Mr. Austen died, his wife and daughters were left without income; had Jane's many brothers not been able to make significant contributions to their upkeep, their situation would have been dire. In her world, Austen could not forget how essential money was for survival.

Contrarily, though, the second lesson Austen learned from her parents was that money—or wealth, rather—was not essential to happiness. The Austens had stories, plays, games, and laughter. If her annual allowance was smaller than she wished, she would have known from the time she was small that one's good humor and one's pocketbook were not inextricably twined, that one could have a wealth of joy without actually being wealthy.

That's not to say that she didn't appreciate wealth. Through her brother Edward and the grand estates he inherited, she came to know that "Elegance & Ease & Luxury" and all they could afford—servants, beautiful things, and delights of every kind. She wrote to Cassandra from Godmersham, "I shall eat Ice & drink French wine & be above Vulgar Economy."[192] And from her home with her parents, she wrote, "People get so horridly poor & economical in this part of the world, that I have no patience with them. Kent [where Edward lived] is the only place for happiness, Everybody is rich there."[193] That "Vulgar Economy" would always have been with Jane, and she would always have expected it to be. The fact that she could temporarily escape it from time to time by visiting her brother in Kent was a gift.

Be careful with those longings.

A couple years into Austen's success as an author, she wrote to her brother Frank, rejoicing to tell him that every copy of *Sense and Sensibility* was sold. (It had taken more than a year and a half since its publication to sell every copy, but still, this was a triumph—especially when Jane had published at her own risk and saved money from her small purse to meet the expected shortfall.) She wrote laughingly to Frank, "I have now therefore written myself into £250.—which only makes me long for more."[194]

I can only imagine that it would have been a huge relief to Austen to have so comparatively large a sum in her hands—equal to what her brothers had together determined to give Mrs. Austen every year for the upkeep of their mother and sisters. But if she did long for more—what author wouldn't?—she knew as well that those sorts of longings needed careful management. Austen's Christian faith taught her as one of its first principles that "the love of money is the root of all evil."[195] More to the point for Austen, perhaps, was the ridiculousness and humor that money-love led to in the world around her. In her novels, she skewers many a character whose greed outpaces every other desire.

Every publishing venture for Austen was a risk—not only the risk every author takes at putting their precious words in the hands of a critical public, but also an actual financial risk. Save for *Pride and Prejudice,* which Jane eventually sold outright to a savvy publisher who knew the book would be successful, she published her books herself and was liable for any losses. She wrote to her niece Fanny about considering a second edition for *Mansfield Park:* "People are more ready to borrow & praise, than to buy—which I cannot wonder at;—but tho' I like praise as well as anybody, I like . . . Pewter too."[196] Unfortunately, that edition would not sell as well as expected, and would lose Austen some of that pewter of hers.

When the second edition of *Sense and Sensibility* came out, she wrote, "I cannot help hoping that *many* will feel themselves obliged to buy it. I shall not mind imagining it a disagreable [*sic*] Duty to them, so as they do it."[197] Anyone who has ever published a book understands Austen's sentiment. But if Austen laughed about being "very greedy & want[ing] to make the most of it,"[198] in regard to her writing, these greedy longings of hers need to be interpreted in light of her own financial obligations. If her books didn't sell, if people chose to "borrow & praise" rather than buy, she could be left with a large debt, possibly even having to go to one of her brothers to have him bail her out. She would certainly have been ashamed and embarrassed if her little hobby, the books she trepidatiously sent out into the world, wound up costing her family money. Luckily, though she lost more than £180 on the second edition of *Mansfield Park,* she had enough earnings to cover that and never had to run to her brothers for help.

Share.

Familiar as Austen was with the elegance of her brother Edward's great estates, she would have known, as well, places similar to the Price family's dirty hovel in Portsmouth as described in *Mansfield Park.* Her knowledge that there were those in greater need, as well as her faith, led her to extend charity. We have an account of her expenses for the year 1807—before she began earning any money from publishing. She spent forty-four pounds total, including nearly fourteen pounds for clothes, nine for washing, six for gifts, and three-and-a-half for charity.[199] Even when her own money was coming largely from others, she gave some of it away. She writes in her letters about buying shifts or other small articles for villagers in need—a trait she passes on to her character Emma, who we see visiting the poor.

Selfishness or stinginess was one of the worst character flaws in Austen's mind. She describes John Dashwood in *Sense and Sensibility:* "He was not an ill-disposed young man, unless to be rather cold hearted, and rather selfish, is to be ill-disposed."[200]

John Dashwood has everything in the world going for him. He inherited a large fortune from his mother, of which he received half upon coming of age. Shortly after that, he married well and increased his bank account further still. Then, in the crisis that opens the story, his great uncle decides to leave the estate of Norland Park in such a way that it must pass to John and his son rather than to Mrs. Dashwood and her three daughters. On his deathbed John's father exacts a promise from him to "do everything in his power to make them comfortable."[201] Mrs. Dashwood and the girls have just £10,000 between them—enough to survive, but a great fall from what they have been accustomed to, and not nearly what their husband and father hoped to give them.

Moved by his father's plea, John determines to give the girls £1,000 each. "Three thousand pounds! he could spare so liberal a sum with little inconvenience,"[202] he thinks. He will get more than that every year from the Norland Park estate. One of the most comical scenes Austen writes regarding money follows his decision. John tells his wife of his plans, and she succeeds in talking him down, saying of his father's request, "He did not know what he was talking of, I dare say; ten to one but he was light-headed at the time. . . . Consider," she says, "that when the money is once parted with, it never can return."[203] First they cut the gift in half, to five hundred pounds apiece, then they think of giving Mrs. Dashwood a small annual annuity instead—but fearing she may live "for ever"[204] since an annuity is owed her, they do away with that idea. They decide that perhaps occasional gifts will be sufficient, until they finally determine that "it is quite absurd to think of" giving them any money at all. In fact, John's wife says, their own needs will be so small, "They will be much more able to give *you* something."[205]

John finally decides to fulfill the promise to his father by helping his stepmother move her furniture when she leaves Norland. But since she moves all the way to Devon, he is unable to help at all and is greatly disturbed to lose this one opportunity he had fixed on for making good on his word. Austen makes him quite ridiculous, and he spends the rest of the novel hemming and hawing about the great financial obligations upon him, so that his stepmother and sisters will not expect anything from him.

Cultivate gratitude.

Jane's brother Henry tells us about her first publishing success:

> *She could scarcely believe what she termed her great good fortune when "Sense and Sensibility" produced a clear profit of about £150. Few so gifted were so truly unpretending. She regarded the above sum as a prodigious recompense for that which had cost her nothing.*[206]

Even in Austen's own day, no doubt, other writers made more money selling lesser works. Her attitude stands out in stark contrast to our own. I think today we expect to make money—and maybe we always expect more. And what we make we certainly see as justified. I question the idea that *Sense and Sensibility* "cost her nothing." She certainly invested her heart in it, an investment not to be made light of. But Austen was grateful, and in Henry's words, "unpretending." It's possible that Henry spoke with the generosity of a brother remembering a loved sister, giving us Austen in her best light. In that light, though, her expectations were small, and her joy big at what she did receive.

Be wise.

Austen took her earnings from her writing and invested them in secure navy 5 percent stock. Perhaps there were occasional splurges, treats for herself and her family, but it seems the bulk of it went straight to the bank. Likely she was thinking of future books and saving up to be able to cover any possible losses—she herself had the foresight that Mr. Bennet in *Pride and Prejudice* lacked. Thinking he would have a son to inherit Longbourn, he failed to save anything from his annual income and could never have afforded to bribe Wickham to marry his daughter Lydia.

Austen joked with Cassandra, "A legacy is our sovereign good,"[207] and "I do not know where we are to get our Legacy, but we will keep a sharp lookout."[208] Rich relations, however, were few, and the one rich uncle who should have given the Austen children substantial legacies in his will ultimately failed to do so (or, rather, left them in such a way that they were of no immediate value). Even when it came to money, ultimately Austen was a realist and would do whatever was in her power to keep herself from overextending. What would she make of the tens of thousands in credit card debt that so many of us carry today? For her, that kind of unsecured spending—buying without actually having money to pay—would have been impossible, and she would have viewed the weight of debt along with the negligence that led to it with horror. (And no doubt as supremely mockable.)

Her letters track her finding the cheaper stores in Bath and spending on things like pink persian, yards of muslin and silk—always with the air of being carefully measured out and considered, as one who is buying the best of what she can afford, but no more, happy to find a bargain when she can. She laments that dresses had to be made up: "I wish such things were to be bought ready made,"[209] she says. She would envy us all the readily available fashion at our fingertips, but what would she make of $700 shoes and $1,000 bags? She would likely be the kind of shopper who favored Target over Neiman Marcus.

Austen could never take her own income for granted. When she published, she didn't know if she would end up making money or owing money, or how much that would even be. And while her brothers did provide some financial support, even their incomes at times were threatened and couldn't be entirely counted on. In that atmosphere of uncertainty and dependence, Austen was careful and grateful, always conscious that her situation could be far worse—and like so many of us, wouldn't entirely have minded making much more.

CHAPTER 10

Seeking Fame and Success

Aside from Austen's chastity, perhaps nothing could separate us from her more than her attitude toward fame. Jane wanted to be successful but she didn't want her name to be known; she preferred her very real, very quiet life. Had someone offered her fifteen minutes of fame, she would have refused. (So many of us today want to be famous even if it's just for being famous—Austen would love the absurdity!)

Before she ever published, Jane wrote in a letter to Cassandra, "I write only for fame, without any view to pecuniary Emolument."[210] She was really just joking about Cassandra's praise of Jane's previous letter (which may have been passed around and admired by friends). In actuality, she would much rather have had that "pecuniary Emolument" than whatever fame the world could give her. All of Austen's books were published without her name on them, carrying the simple line "By A Lady." When her first novel, *Sense and Sensibility,* came out, some advertisements misprinted it as being "By Lady A—," which started some speculation about who exactly this "Lady

A" was.[211] Of course they actually were by a "Lady A," though that particular lady tried to withhold her name from the public as long as she could.

The inner circle of her family knew her secret and also knew that she wanted to have that secret kept, but her brother Henry—winsome and impulsive—could not oblige. After his wife died, Henry took his eldest nephew with him on a trip to Scotland, where they heard *Pride and Prejudice* praised by Lady Robert Kerr and her friend. Though he couldn't admit it to his quiet sister, Henry told his niece Fanny that he had enlightened Lady Robert about who wrote the book she was admiring. Jane wrote, "He told her with as much satisfaction as if it were my wish."[212] She then explained the situation in a letter to Frank, giving us as much as we know of her thoughts on fame:

> *The truth is that the Secret has spread so far as to be scarcely the Shadow of a secret now—& that I beleive [*sic*] whenever the 3d appears, I shall not even attempt to tell Lies about it. . . . Henry heard P. & P. warmly praised in Scotland . . . & what does he do in the warmth of his Brotherly vanity & Love, but immediately tell them who wrote it!—A Thing once set going in that way—one knows how it spreads!—and he, dear Creature, has set it going so much more than once. I know it is all done from affection & partiality—but at the same time, let me here again express to you & Mary my sense of the* superior *kindness which you have shewn on the occasion, in doing what I wished.—I am*

> *trying to harden myself.—After all, what a trifle it is in all its Bearings, to the really important points of one's existence even in this World!*[213]

Whether the last sentence was written with a sly grin or not is impossible to tell, but Austen seems genuinely bothered that her secret got out. It's such a telling little story, of the admiring older brother who couldn't help divulging his sister's success. For Henry, to hear Jane's writing praised and not have people know that it was by his own sister was too much to bear. Whether he told out of a desire for Jane to be known, or for his own reputation, to be known as being related to that talented writer—or more likely a mixture of motivations—ultimately, Jane couldn't help but forgive him. When her third book, *Mansfield Park,* came out, she decided she wouldn't deny having written it—perhaps she had been forced into lies in the past, having to deny authorship of *Sense and Sensibility* and *Pride and Prejudice.* But not denying something is far different from openly admitting it. Simply because her secret was out didn't mean that she had to help spread it. She would continue to publish in anonymity and try to "harden" herself to anyone knowing that she was the author of those lovely books.

Given our fame-obsessed world, her attitude is so striking. For Austen, the idea of fame, the possibility of rumors, was enough to cause distress. When she writes, "what a trifle it is," she may be referring to her own pain at the disclosure or she could be referring to fame itself, "a trifle" compared "to the really important points of one's existence."

Don't equate fame with importance or success.

We are prone to think of fame as an end in itself, perhaps as the greatest proof of one's importance. For Austen, though, success and fame were two very different things. Because of the tradition of anonymous publishing, she could hope to be a successful writer without ever even being known—something few of us would desire.

Austen did achieve a moderate amount of success in her lifetime. Though the largest print run of any of her novels was most likely *Emma*'s two thousand copies, her books tended to sell out, which was an accomplishment then—and still is today, as authors struggle to sell through their print runs and hope for more. She received good reviews and set the literary world talking. Various writers were given credit for her novels, some of whom were not at all eager to dispel the rumors. And she gathered a lofty readership, including members of the royal family and society's elite.

Reviewers gave *Sense and Sensibility* "particular commendation,"[214] and when *Pride and Prejudice* was published, the reviews were glowing. Among others, *The British Critic* called it "far superior to almost all the publications of the kind which have lately come before us."[215] If Austen was unknown, she had been noticed by the literary world, which must have been very gratifying. Playwright Richard Sheridan said the book was "one of the cleverest things he ever read," and Austen scholar Deirdre Le Faye believes that "*Pride and Prejudice* became the fashionable novel for the spring of 1813."[216] Whether Austen knew that is questionable, but she probably got some sense of her growing reputation from her well-connected brother Henry. Her friend Anne Sharp even wrote with "sweet flattery" to tell her she was "read and admired in Ireland too"[217] and that at least one lady among her acquaintance very much wanted to know about the author.

Austen wanted to know that she had done well and collected opinions of family and friends about her books, delineating who liked which one best—even the occasional neighbor who didn't like them much at all. She loved hearing warm praise from family friend Warren Hastings, a politician who had served as the first Governor-General of India, who admired her Elizabeth Bennet "so much."[218] Her brother Charles wrote home with kind words from a naval officer friend who had no idea that Charles's sister was the author of the much-loved *Sense and Sensibility* and *Pride and Prejudice* and the less well-liked *Mansfield Park*. Austen felt sympathy with only a tiny hint of wounded pride when one of her niece Fanny's gentlemen friends did not take well to her novels; he had been goaded by Fanny into reading them and giving his opinion, but she neglected to tell him who the author was, which Jane thought was rather unfair. Jane wrote: "I *hope* I am not affronted & do not think the worse of him for having a Brain so very different than mine."[219] She welcomed praise from those at every level, but didn't need everyone to love her books.

When *Emma* was released, Walter Scott wrote about it anonymously for *Quarterly Review.* Scott was one of Austen's favorite writers—she only disdained that he should write novels in addition to poetry and thereby creep into her territory. If only Austen knew that it was her beloved Scott who praised her as being almost in a class by herself for capturing daily life in so captivating a manner. "Keeping close to common incidents, and to such characters as occupy the ordinary walks of life," he wrote, "she has produced sketches of such spirit and originality."[220]

At this point, Austen's fame was a growing flame: People were interested. They loved her books and wanted to know who she was. The fact that she could get a sense of this—though she couldn't know the full extent of it—and completely turn aside says a great deal about who she was. She could have fed it, made the most of it, had some kind of public life, like other writers of the day. But she was content—happy—to be unknown. She laughed with her sister about having her portrait done and put on display, saying, "I do not despair of having my picture in the Exhibition at last."[221] In truth, though, nothing could have distressed her more.

Choose substance over celebrity.

Had Austen wanted celebrity, she did have one opportunity she could have capitalized on. When Henry became dangerously ill before *Emma* was published, one of his doctors happened to also serve as one of the Prince Regent's doctors. Austen's authorship had become generally known, at least among Henry's circles, so Henry's doctor "informed her one day that the Prince was a great admirer of her novels; that he read them often, and kept a set in every one of his residences; that he himself therefore had thought it right to inform his Royal Highness that Miss Austen was staying in London."[222] The result was that Dr. Clarke, the Prince's librarian, came to see Jane and invited her to visit the Prince's residence at Carlton House. Nothing could have seemed more unlikely—or perhaps more distasteful—to Jane. She detested the Prince Regent, as so many did, for his licentious extravagance. As lofty as his title, it's doubtful she would have wanted him among her admirers—or expected him to be one of them, given the tame stories she told.

Austen paid the visit to opulent Carlton House, where she was invited to dedicate her next book to the prince. She most likely would have chosen to decline but understood the invitation to be more of a command, and she also hoped the dedication would help accelerate the sluggish printers, who were running behind. The event occasioned a correspondence between Austen and Dr. Clarke, which she must have found comical. Clarke encouraged her "to delineate in some future Work the Habits of Life and Character and enthusiasm of a Clergyman—who should pass his time between the metropolis & the Country,"[223] and then gives further details of his own life for inspiration. Jane begged off, claiming to be incapable of the task, being "with all possible Vanity, the most unlearned, & uninformed Female who ever dared to be an Authoress."[224] In another letter, Clarke boldly encouraged her, "Pray continue to write, & make all your friends send Sketches to help you"[225]—as if Austen had any need of help!

Clarke seemed anxious to know Jane better, but she skillfully declined and went back to her quiet life, so similar to the "pictures of domestic Life in Country Villages"[226] she wrote about. She didn't want a life about court, having or pretending to have friends in high places with all the frippery and nonsense that involved. She might have loved the laugh it gave her, but she couldn't live there.

Don't be afraid of a small life.

While we may look to fame for significance, Austen found meaning in the things that seem smaller to us—in her relationships with family and friends; in being a daughter, sister, aunt. Her quiet perch in the countryside was where she wanted to be, a place she imbued with significance by living fully and well, and by telling the stories it kindled—doing the work that brimmed up out of an active imagination and a full heart. The very quietness and smallness of that life might inspire fear in us—fear of not being significant or big enough—but for Austen, it was inspiration itself.

Chapter 11

Venturing Solo

We associate Jane Austen with happily-ever-after, so it comes as quite a surprise to learn that she never married. I doubt she ever stopped hoping for love or being open to that possibility, but her own life didn't mirror her stories. Ironically, Austen, our patron saint of romance, can teach us something about being single.

If Jane didn't marry, she still inspired a great deal of interest. In addition to her young flirtation with Tom Lefroy, and the proposal she ultimately rejected from the very eligible Harris Bigg-Wither, she seems to have received at least one more proposal. The details are lost to us, but it appears that Edward Bridges, the brother-in-law of her own brother Edward, made an offer of marriage probably when Jane was twenty-nine. In a later letter, Jane makes a cryptic reference to not having been able to accept his "invitation"[227] and rejoices when he marries someone else. All we really know about Edward Bridges is that he once ordered "toasted cheese for supper entirely on [Jane's] account"[228]—but apparently such offerings were not enough to stir her heart. And when Jane was in her mid-thirties, her brother Henry's lawyer,

Mr. Seymour, is thought to have asked Henry for permission to propose. After contemplating it, though, Mr. Seymour decided not to go through with it—perhaps Jane gave him no encouragement—which would have made their further dealings a bit awkward.

Austen somehow found balance, peace, and joy being both the writer of beautiful if improbable love stories and also being a woman who never married. It would have been easy for her to go to one extreme or the other. She could have written romantic stories (really, her books are so much more than this—as she said, "I could not sit seriously down to write a serious Romance under any other motive than to save my Life"[229]) and been so consumed with them that she could derive happiness from nothing else, in fiction or in real life—in which case, her writing would have made her happy but her life would have made her miserable. Or she could have gone to the opposite extreme and renounced romance entirely when she discovered that it wasn't going to come her way—in which case she would either never have published or would have published much different sorts of books and would have lost the joy of those lovely stories. Remarkably, she did both, which really is no small feat. Honestly, it's inspiring.

Treasure the roles you are given.

If Jane was never a mother, she adored being an aunt. She was never a distant, unknown relation in this role; she knew her many nieces and nephews intimately. When they were small, she played games and make-believe with them, told them fairy stories that would go on for days (it seems a tragedy those were never written down), and was their general favorite. Her niece Caroline remembered, "As a very little girl, I was always creeping up to her, and following her whenever I could . . . Her charm to children was great sweetness of manner—she seemed to love you, and you loved her naturally in return."[230] Of nearly three-year-old George, Edward's third child, Jane wrote, "I flatter myself that *itty Dordy* will not forget me . . . Kiss him for me."[231] And when an older William decided to make a footstool for his aunts and grandmother at Chawton, Jane said, "We shall never have the heart to put our feet upon it."[232] As an aunt, she was certainly sweet and doting, if never so blind that she couldn't assess her nieces' and nephews' faults.

Jane's eldest niece was Edward's daughter Fanny. By the time she was fifteen, Jane regarded her as "almost another Sister." Surprised by the depth of this connection, she says that she "could not have supposed that a niece would ever have been so much to me. She is quite after one's own heart."[233] As Fanny's mother died within days of that letter being written, aunt and niece were destined to be closer still. Years later, as Fanny was pouring out her heart to her Aunt Jane seeking advice on love, Jane would write:

> *You are inimitable, irrresistable [*sic*]. You are the delight of my Life. . . . Such a description of your queer little heart! . . . You are worth your weight in Gold. . . . It is very, very gratifying to me to know you so intimately.*[234]

Aunt Jane also gave writing advice to her brother James's three children. She read their stories and gave them thoughtful critiques with abundant praise. (One can't help but be jealous at the wealth of talent at their disposal.) She calls James-Edward's stories "strong, manly, spirited Sketches, full of Variety & Glow."[235] And she was just as happy about who he turned out to be, to "see the sweet temper and warm affections of the Boy confirmed in the young Man."[236] In niece Anna's story, her hero St. Julian was in love with Cecilia's aunt before falling in love with Cecilia. Austen had fun with this, writing in jest about Anna's husband Ben, "I rather imagine indeed that Neices [*sic*] are seldom chosen but in complement to some Aunt or other. I dare say Ben was in love with me once, & wd never have thought of *You* if he had not supposed me dead of a Scarlet fever."[237]

Austen wanted her nieces and nephews to succeed, even if it was in her own area of talent. And she worried about their well-being. When Anna first became engaged to Ben, she feared that their personalities were too unstable and too different for lifelong happiness together. She laughed with Cassandra that Ben might choose to pay a visit when both Jane and Cassandra—"the formidables"[238]—were away. A potential suitor might have wanted to avoid those two protective aunts.

Not being married and not having her own family gave Jane the freedom to invest her time and love as an aunt. It was certainly something she cherished. As Emma predicts to Harriet Smith of her own expected singleness, "I shall be very well off, with all the children of a sister I love so much, to care about. There will be enough of them . . . for every hope and fear . . . My nephews and nieces!—I shall often have a niece with me."[239] Our own cherished roles may be quite different than Aunt Jane's, with all those "nephews and nieces!"—and different than we ever expected.

Enjoy your freedom.

Austen would have recognized her great freedom in being unmarried, more than we could today. Marriage then, without readily available birth control, meant constant, youth-draining "breeding,"[240] as Austen called it. While she loved her nieces and nephews, there's enough in her letters to make one believe that she wouldn't have been nearly as thrilled to have a large brood of her own. When George ("itty Dordy") was about nine months old, she wrote, "I have taken little George once in my arms . . . which I thought very kind."[241] Perhaps she was less inclined to like babies and more inclined to like children who could walk and talk—who could enjoy games and stories.

Her niece Anna married at twenty-one and had two children in rapid succession. With children around eighteen months and six months, she appeared to be pregnant again, which spurred Jane to write: "Anna has not a chance of escape. . . . Poor Animal, she will be worn out before she is thirty.—I am very sorry for her. . . . I am quite tired of so many Children."[242] Austen must have felt her own precious escape from a life of regular bearing and begetting—the kind of life that reminded her of the animals on her father's farm.

There were other sweetnesses in the solitary life as well. Upon spending some time with only her mother at home, Jane wrote to Cassandra about their dear friend Martha's expected return, "I am now got into such a way of being alone that I do not wish even for her."[243] Whatever precious time she enjoyed alone would have been nonexistent had she had a family. It was to her one of the "comforts of being . . . single,"[244] which her friend Harriot Bridges regretted leaving behind when she married. Jane could not feel sorry for Harriot, whose great difficulty was that she couldn't enjoy being married and single at the same time, that the benefits of one were different than the other and couldn't both be had at once.

At nearly thirty-eight, Jane wrote of an evening party with her niece Fanny: "By the bye, as I must leave off being young, I find many Douceurs in being a sort of Chaperon for I am put on the Sofa near the Fire and can drink as much wine as I like."[245] It's possible that her marital status had nothing to do with her ability to sit by the fire drinking wine, but a single Aunt Jane must have been a welcome chaperone, her sharp eye taking in everything to be discussed later with her effusive wit and spirit.

Embrace your gifts.

One thing probably spared Jane a lot of the pain she might otherwise have felt at not ever meeting her great love: She had a gift. She had stories to tell. They were her love, her "own darling Child[ren],"[246] dear and precious. The time she might have spent managing a large household and keeping up with a passel of children instead went to crafting narratives and shaping dialogue. The joy of bearing her own flesh and blood (if that would have been a joy to her) was substituted with a different kind of bearing—one belonging to the mind rather than the body, borne of her own keen imagination. And one which we can't doubt brought her deep joy.

Given Austen's *joie de vivre* and her hesitance to linger in disappointment, it's fair to say that she didn't put a lot of energy into yearning for what wasn't to be, even if that loss touched a fragile spot in her heart. Her energy, her life, would have been invested in the delicate art of creating. As she talked about her work, she likened it to working on a "little bit (two Inches wide) of Ivory . . . with so fine a Brush as produces little effect after much labour."[247] But that was the careful work she loved, what she called "the delight of my life;—3 or 4 families in a Country Village."[248] After her family and small group of friends, the balance of her affection went to her stories. Whatever romantic experiences she had—both humorous and tragic—fed and fueled her writing.

It's possible that Austen's singleness may have been *our* gift rather than hers. At the time of that romance with the charming unnamed man by the sea, the one that ended with his tragic death, none of her books had been published, and three of them were not even conceived. Had she married then, there's a good chance that she couldn't have been bothered with things like negotiating with publishers and correcting page proofs; her life could have eclipsed her writing and cut her work short. She may never have been published and never written more. Had Austen married, we might not know her name at all. As she told Cassandra after managing their small household in Cassandra's absence, "Composition seems to me Impossible, with a head full of Joints of Mutton & doses of rhubarb."[249] How poor would we be then, had Austen traded in Pemberley and Barton for meals and washing!

Alas, we can't expect to share Austen's great giftedness, but we can direct our energy toward pursuing our own smaller gifts, whatever those may be.

Don't live life alone.

Austen was alone, romantically, but she was rarely ever actually alone. She never lived by herself, and the household she shared with her mother, sister, and Martha had a regular rotation of visitors—so much so that Jane was often ready for them to leave. It's hardly the way we would live today, with our much greater independence. For Jane it presented challenges. Austen's time was not entirely at her disposal. She couldn't determine when family visits were arranged, and when she wanted to travel she was largely dependent on her brothers taking her and picking her up—which meant that her schedule at times depended on their whims. She was also dependent on her brothers financially. She was painfully aware that without her family, she would have been in a fair way to be indigent, like *Emma*'s loquacious Miss Bates. "Single women have a dreadful propensity for being poor,"[250] she wrote.

By contrast, nowadays there's little we can't do on our own, foremost earning our own keep. Austen would rejoice in that progress—that singleness is no longer equated with poverty is surely a great good. But what we've gained in independence, perhaps we've lost in community. I doubt that Austen was lonely much. She was surrounded by a rich circle of family and friends with whom she experienced life. If some of those family and friends could grate at times, together they provided a great deal of love and meaning. Depending on them for survival may have been occasionally awkward, but in their loving family this largely bound them together instead of driving them apart. Austen never read a book without discussing it with someone, never celebrated a holiday alone, rarely laughed without sharing the joke. Where we have whole houses to ourselves and often communicate through cyberspace, Austen shared a room with her dear sister for her whole life.

Singleness didn't equal isolation for Austen. Our challenge may be not to allow our wonderful independence to make us so autonomous that we forget we need other people. Austen's life is a reminder to build community and invest in those close to us, and to cherish the love we're given—whether it's from older brothers or little nieces and nephews, or from our own family of friends.

Stay open.

Perhaps Austen reached a point at which she became settled in her spinsterhood and ceased to hope for anything else. Maybe sometime in her thirties she became happily resigned to her fate. I don't know, but I like to think that she remained open—that the author of these wonderful stories of hope in hopeless situations always had a tinge of expectation and never entirely quashed her romantic dreams. If she did give up, perhaps it was not because she despaired of being sought but because she found no one she could love. She joked after one ball, "There was a scarcity of Men in general, & a still greater scarcity of any that were good for much."[251]

What we do know is that she stayed open to life and embraced the unexpected goodness it brought her. Her publishing success was everything she could have wanted it to be. She certainly never imagined that she would be summoned to the Prince Regent's home or invited to dedicate a book to him. The glowing reviews her stories received in national publications must have been very gratifying. Maybe this is the point at which she would tell us that embracing life is just that—that living a joy-filled life alone doesn't mean you are closing yourself off to any possibilities, it simply means that you relish life and its goodness, regardless of marital status, which may or may not change.

She was wise enough to understand that some would have a harder time with this than others. She told her niece Fanny, "I do wish you to marry very much, because I know you will never be happy til you are."[252] But for Austen, being single was not an excuse to shut down and withdraw, or to cease being happy.

Thrive.

One December, Jane went to a ball in Southampton with Martha. Jane danced with an acquaintance with lovely black eyes, but he seems to have spoken only French, so she concluded that "his black eyes may be the best of him." She would write later to Cassandra, "It was the same room in which we danced 15 years ago!—I thought it all over—& inspite of the shame of being so much older, felt with thankfulness that I was quite as happy now as then."[253] She was then weeks away from turning thirty-three. Fifteen years prior, she would have been seventeen or eighteen, full of dreams and likely romantic expectations. The fact that she was still "quite as happy" tells me that however differently her life may have turned out from what she expected, it was not to her disliking. She had a recipe for a full life—exploring her gifts, cherishing and returning the love of her nieces and nephews, investing in those around her, telling good stories.

Single women take many forms in Austen's stories, from the dour, wealthy Lady Catherine de Bourgh to the impoverished, effusive Miss Bates. The one character who welcomes singleness, who fully expects to be an old maid, is Emma, and her conversation with Harriet about that prospect (written when Austen was in her late thirties) is striking. Emma tells Harriet:

> *I . . . have very little intention of ever marrying at all. . . . I must see somebody very superior to any one I have seen yet, to be*

> *tempted; . . . and I do* not *wish to see any such person. . . . If I were to marry, I must expect to repent it.*

She goes on to explain that her situation is ideal. She has fortune and employment. She is essentially mistress of Hartfield. And she has never been (and never expects to be) in love. Harriet is aghast: "But still, you will be an old maid! and that's so dreadful!" Emma replies:

> *Never mind, Harriet, I shall not be a poor old maid; . . . A single woman, with a very narrow income, must be a ridiculous, disagreeable, old maid! . . . but a single woman, of good fortune, is always respectable, and may be as sensible and pleasant as anybody else.*[254]

How much Emma is echoing Austen's own thoughts is unknown—maybe Austen herself was still waiting to "see somebody very superior" and maybe she thought marriage could bring regret. But Austen found her own way to be a dreadful old maid—and not a wealthy one—while still being "as sensible and pleasant as anybody else." Even in that she shows something of a fierce independent streak, determined to make of her life what she would, whatever society thought of her.

It's worth noting that Austen chose not to have any of her heroines remain unmarried—even Emma, with all of her single aspirations. No matter her own happiness and the goodness she found in her unmarried state, it couldn't provide the joyful resolution she wanted for her novels. Maybe she understood as well, that spinsters, however happy, wouldn't sell books. An Elizabeth Bennet who remained single with her family at Longbourn probably wouldn't be much talked about today, but a Mrs. Darcy—a Mrs. Darcy was a powerful thing.

So Austen continued that delicate balance, her lovely stories with their perfect endings, paired with her life, whose ending—whose substance—she was continuing to craft as she went. If she lived today she would never be the kind of single woman who stayed sadly in the dark and collected cats. Single or not, Jane Austen thrived.

Chapter 12

Enduring the Hardest Things

If Austen's life sounds somewhat idyllic, it wasn't without its doses of pain. She loved her life in the quiet countryside and faced one of her first tragedies at twenty-five when she lost her beloved childhood home as her parents decided to retire and move to Bath. Part of the struggle of being ever dependent was having no say in where the family lived, and it seems that neither Jane nor her sister were consulted. Jane had been visiting good friend Martha Lloyd and her mother. When she and Martha returned to the Austens in their little village of Steventon, they were welcomed by Mrs. Austen's: "Well, girls, it is all settled, we have decided to leave Steventon in such a week and go to Bath."[255] It was the first hint Jane had of the significant change. Family tradition says that she was so shocked she fainted—though it's hard to imagine her ever losing control to that extent.

There's a theory among those who study Austen's life that living in Bath depressed Jane so much that she was unable to write. It's true that she must have ached for the country she loved so dearly, where she knew the paths and trees and eagerly watched the seasons. And she would have missed her close circle of intimates. The greatest nuisance of Bath, though, may have been all the acquaintances that Jane could have done without, along with the endless parties. Mrs. Austen's wealthy brother and his wife, Jane's aunt and uncle Leigh-Perrot, were in Bath, and by necessity the Austens were woven into their larger social circle. Jane wrote to Cassandra, "another stupid party last night,"[256] and "I hate tiny parties—they force one into constant exertion."[257] It wasn't just the parties, but the people themselves, who taxed Jane. "I cannot anyhow continue to find people agreable [*sic*],"[258] she wrote. Jane had less time for herself, and less time for her writing, and she was devoting more time to people she didn't care so much about.

If Bath was a place of annoyance it also became a place of great sadness. On December 16,1804, Jane's twenty-ninth birthday, her dear friend Anne Lefroy was killed in the Hampshire countryside in a tragic riding accident. Mrs. Lefroy was an excellent rider, but her horse was giving her problems and may have been spooked; her servant exacerbated the situation when he tried to ride up and grab the reins. She fell or threw herself from the horse and died later that day. Anne had been friend and mentor to Jane. She was educated, cultivated, literary, and determined, like the Austens, to live out her Christian faith in a meaningful way. Four years later and still mourning her loss, Austen wrote the only truly serious poem by her that survives, wishing that she could see her friend's face again for one brief moment, recalling the "bitter pang of torturing Memory!" of losing Mrs. Lefroy on her own birthday and describing her as an "Angelic Woman! past my power to praise."[259]

Anne Lefroy's death was followed quickly by Mr. Austen's. He was then nearly seventy-five and had started to struggle a bit, but his death came as a shock. Jane described him as being "seized . . . with a return of the feverish complaint, which he had been subject to for the three last years." He seemed to recover, only to quickly decline beyond hope of recovery. She wrote, "It has been very sudden!—within twenty four hours of his death he was walking with only the help of a stick, was even reading!" Along with her siblings, she mourned her "Excellent Father."[260] These Bath years were also the time when Jane would have met that charming, unnamed suitor during one of her seaside vacations. Their courtship would also end with his tragic death.

While the Austen sons quickly stepped in with financial help, Mrs. Austen and the girls didn't have a home and spent nearly two years paying visits to various family members and renting short-term places in Bath before they were able to settle with Frank and his new wife in Southampton. With her unwelcome social obligations, followed by this kind of grief and years of being unsettled, it's little wonder that Austen didn't produce much from Bath and the period that followed. Her great struggle, though, was yet to come, nearly a decade later.

Austen had always been full of energy—the aunt playing endless games, the "desperate walker," the ball-goer who could write, "There were twenty Dances & I danced them all,

& without any fatigue. . . I fancy I could just as well dance for a week together."[261] She also seems to have been remarkably healthy, aside from a dangerous brush with typhoid fever as a child. But sometime after her fortieth birthday, she began to feel unwell. Again, the picture we have here is murky, but she had some back pain, feverish nights, rheumatism—or pain, and "bile," which probably signifies some kind of intestinal difficulties. Full-of-life Jane now began a lengthy journey with a mysterious chronic illness.

The fact that all of this began around her fortieth birthday may have been due to stress: The Austen family had suffered one tragedy after another. Her brother Charles's young wife died at twenty-four after giving birth to her fourth child. One of his young daughters was diagnosed with having water on the brain and had to endure experimental treatments to try to cure her. Successful Henry went bankrupt, losing £20,000 of Edward's fortune in the process. After Charles went back to sea, his boat was shipwrecked in the Mediterranean, leaving him to stand trial for something for which he was blameless. Edward's estates had come under attack from neighbors who were suing him, claiming that a generations-old break of entails had been incorrectly done, and that they should be the ones to inherit his Hampshire properties. (Had that lawsuit, which dragged on for years, been successful, Mrs. Austen and her daughters would have had to leave their comfortable home at Chawton Cottage.) Stress and heartbreak abounded, which may have weakened Jane to the point of susceptibility, or allowed something that had already compromised her system to gain the upper hand. For the next year and a half, she would face this with the grace and spirit that characterized her life.

Be honest.

Jane wrote to family members with unflinching honesty about her health. She didn't evade or deny, she simply stated the facts and moved on. Being Austen, of course, she didn't have any of the kind of false humility that would lead her to try to entirely cover something like this up, to pretend it didn't exist and thereby end up ultimately making something bigger of it. No—it simply was, and it would be discussed as such.

She told Cassandra on a good day, "My Back has given me scarcely any pain for many days."[262] Invited to dine with her niece Anna and her little family, she wrote to nephew James-Edward that she was forced to decline, because "the walk is beyond my strength."[263] As she got worse, she said more. She would admit to Fanny:

> *I certainly have not been well for many weeks, & about a week ago I was very poorly, I have had a good deal of fever at times & indifferent nights, but am considerably better now, & recovering my Looks a little, which have been bad enough, black & white & every wrong colour. I must not depend on being ever very blooming again.*[264]

She would not flinch even from something so delicate as her own loss of beauty, the strange symptom of her illness, which brought alternating patches of light and dark to her skin. She would tell her little niece Caroline, "[In] short I am a poor Honey at present."[265]

Typical of Austen, these are small bits in the midst of otherwise lengthy letters about family news, often tucked in between advice to her nephews and nieces on love or writing.

Don't indulge.

The writer who created hypochondriacs Mrs. Bennet and Mary Elliot Musgrove could not indulge in her own sickness, however real. It must have given her some pain to acknowledge her illness at all. She wrote of one family friend, "She is a poor Honey—the sort of woman who gives me the idea of being determined never to be well—& who likes her spasms & nervousness & the consequence they give her, better than anything else."[266] If Austen was going to be a "poor Honey," she was not going to be *that* kind of poor Honey, the kind that enjoyed the attention she got simply for being sick, that wanted to linger there a while. It's fair to say that *Pride and Prejudice*'s Mrs. Bennet, upstairs in her houserobe, making the most of her imaginary symptoms, couldn't have been further from Austen herself.

Even at just forty, with her mother almost twice her age, Austen wrote, "Sickness is a dangerous Indulgence at my time of Life."[267] It was dangerous. And, no, she would not indulge.

Maintain hope.

Every time Austen wrote about her illness, she saw some reason to be optimistic—some sign that she was going to recover and be, if not fully well, at least better. This may have had more to do with her own determination rather than the illness itself, though as her symptoms waxed and waned she eagerly watched them for glimpses of progress. She would write to Caroline, "*I* feel myself getting stronger than I was half a year ago, & can so perfectly well walk to Alton, *or* back again, without the slightest fatigue that I hope to be able to do both when summer comes."[268] She was continually making plans to be better. Every energy was directed to health rather than sickness.

Though no doctor knew how to diagnose or treat Jane's illness, she hoped to manage it herself. She told her friend Alethea Bigg: "I . . . am not far from being well; & I think I understand my own case now so much better than I did, as to be able by care to keep off any serious return of illness."[269] To Fanny she wrote, "I am almost entirely cured of my rheumatism; just a little pain in my knee now & then, to make me remember what it was."[270]

As one would expect of Austen, she maintained her sense of humor throughout, even regarding her illness. She knew that to laugh was to diminish the power of the thing. She told Cassandra, "I am nursing myself up now into as beautiful a state as I can, because I hear that Dr White means to call on me."[271] Leave it to Jane to laugh about flirting from her sickbed. Even when forced to leave for Winchester, to be under the care of doctors there, she could smile about being "a very genteel, portable sort of Invalid."[272]

Fight against it.

If Austen was going to be forced to succumb to this, she was determined that it would be against her every effort. In addition to setting her mind and heart against it, she was continually making plans for how she could get the better of it—walking as much as she could, and when unable to do that, she would use her little donkey carriage or even just ride the donkeys themselves (though she laughed about the donkeys being difficult and having "forgotten much of their Education"[273]). Though forced to rest more than she would like, forced to stay in bed, she was determined to move toward health wherever possible. Her precious country walks were what she most wanted. As the weather turned to spring, she wrote, "I am got tolerably well again, quite equal to walking about & enjoying the Air; & by sitting down & resting a good while between my Walks, I get exercise enough."[274] Such a desperate walker as Jane had to be outside, even if it meant resting and walking in equal measure. Those who have dealt with chronic illness will understand the kind of courage and strength this takes, to not just lay down and give up, but to always continue trying, however small your successes may be, and despite being dogged daily by exhaustion and fatigue.

Allow it to mold your temperament.

In the midst of this sickness, Austen was finishing *Persuasion,* where she tells the story of poor Mrs. Smith's struggles with the rheumatism that temporarily crippled her. She writes with admiration of Mrs. Smith's temperament—"the choicest gift of Heaven"—which enabled her to find joy when everything in her life had gone wrong. Remarkably, she has not become bitter. She has buried her husband, lost her money, has no family, and not much health, but "she had moments only of languor and depression, to hours of occupation and enjoyment."[275] Perhaps for Mrs. Smith this gifted nature was innate; most of us have to work to get there. Austen's temperament was probably close to that of Mrs. Smith—her letters read as though the "hours of enjoyment" outweighed occasional "moments of depression"—but with her critical eye she probably felt that she still had need of being refined and would have seen her own illness as the opportunity to develop the sort of resilience she admired.

Let others care for you.

However great Austen's hopes and her resolve, her body continued to grow weak, her illness thrived. By April of 1817 she would take a dramatic turn, and even after a brief reprieve, wrote, "I live upstairs however for the present & am coddled."[276] Late in the month, in secret, she wrote her will, leaving almost everything to her sister. In May she left her home for the care of

Dr. Lyford in Winchester. Cassandra went with her to take care of her, and she had a constant rotation of brothers visiting.

Even still, she continued to hope. She wrote from Winchester to her dear nephew James-Edward, "I continue to get better. . . . I am gaining strength very fast. I am now out of bed from 9 in the morn^{g} to 10 at night—Upon the Sopha [*sic*] t'is true—but I . . . can employ myself, & walk from one room to another." Her spirit wasn't weak—she told James-Edward that Dr. Lyford had promised to cure her, and that if he did not, she would "draw up a Memorial [a petition] & lay it before the Dean & Chapter, & have no doubt of redress from that Pious, Learned & disinterested Body."[277] (This would be like saying that if she died, she would sue for damages.)

Being "coddled" was a difficult thing for Austen, as she was used to being the one taking care of those around her. To be taken care of was entirely different. To her good friend Anne Sharp she would write:

> *How to do justice to the kindness of all my family during this illness, is quite beyond me!—Every dear Brother so affectionate & so anxious!—And as for my Sister!—Words must fail me in any attempt to describe what a Nurse she has been to me.*[278]

But as always, she couldn't stay terribly serious for long. Further on, she said, "In short, if I live to be an old Woman I must expect to wish I had died now, blessed in the tenderness of such a Family, & before I had survived either them or their affection."[279]

She didn't feel worthy of all that family love, the warmth and constancy of which brought her to tears.

Be grateful.

The other theme running through Austen's letters of this time is gratitude. She told Anne Sharp, "I have so many alleviations & comforts to bless the Almighty for!"[280] Not least was her family, but she was also thankful to rarely have been in pain. With her failing body, with hopes of a healing she knew might not come, Austen was still overwhelmed at the goodness around her.

We can assume that this is how she continued those summer months—her final months—at Winchester: spirited, gracious, brave. "With all the Egotism of an Invalid I write only of myself,"[281] she wrote to Anne. But no one who reads her letters could think that was the case. Even in her final illness, Austen strove to get outside of herself, to be that loving sister, friend, and aunt.

Dr. Lyford as much as admitted to the family that Jane would not recover. When James saw her in June, he thought she was "well aware of her situation."[282] One of the hardest things—for all involved—must have been that the illness didn't steadily get worse, rather it continued to lift from time to time, continuing to give some hope of a recovery. In early June, Jane thought she was dying, to be spared by another reprieve. But in mid-July she came to the end. She grew visibly weaker before she had what Cassandra described as a seizure—her doctor thought perhaps a blood vessel burst. Cassandra wrote:

> *She felt herself to be dying about half an hour before she became tranquil & aparently* [sic] *unconscious. During that half hour was her struggle, poor Soul! she said she could not tell us what she sufferd* [sic], *tho she complaind* [sic] *of little fixed pain. When I asked her if there was any thing she wanted, her answer was she wanted nothing but death & some of her words were "God grant me patience, Pray for me Oh Pray for me."*[283]

At half past four in the morning of July 18, Jane died, her head on a pillow supported by her sister Cassandra. She was forty-one.

Jane's mother, her brothers, nieces and nephews, and especially Cassandra, mourned their loss. But perhaps one great comfort was that they did not mourn who Jane had been, that they could celebrate her life and how she lived. They wrote the epitaph for her grave in Winchester, which reads in part:

> *The benevolence of her heart, the sweetness of her temper, and the extraordinary endowments of her mind obtained the regard of all who knew her, and the warmest love of her intimate connections. Their grief is in proportion to their affection, they know their loss to be irreparable, but in their deepest affliction*

they are consoled by a firm though humble hope that her charity, devotion, faith and purity have rendered her soul acceptable in the sight of her REDEEMER.

As lovely as they thought her, as talented as they knew her to be, they would be shocked to know that we mourn her still, that her adoring fans still grieve that she did not live to write more. Almost a decade later, Walter Scott would write in his journal, "What a pity such a gifted creature died so early!"[284] In her grief, consumed with thoughts of her sister, Cassandra wrote, "I know the time must come when my mind will be less engrossed by her idea, but I do not like to think of it."[285] Yet today we are engrossed by her still.

Chapter 13

Finding Joy and Laughter

Jane Austen was buoyant. She lived with energy and joy. It's impossible to read her letters and books without coming away with the sense that she was something of an irrepressible force. She laughed at herself, at the everyday world, and at everyone around her (mostly all in good fun)—and she welcomed having them all laugh at her. But if she relished laughter, there was more to that vital spirit of hers. She wrote to Cassandra of a ball at which she had "had an odd set of partners": "I had a very pleasant evening, however, though you will probably find out that there was no particular reason for it; but I do not think it worth while to wait for enjoyment until there is some real opportunity for it."[286] So she did not "wait for enjoyment," she simply took joy wherever she could, and as much as possible.

Greet the world with energy.

I think Austen could give classes on loving life. She was engaged, even in small things. Daily concerns were not below her wit or interest. She could laugh about needing to repair her hat—"on which You know my principal hopes of happiness depend," she wrote[287]—and tell Cassandra, "You know how interesting the purchase of a sponge-cake is to me."[288] She had a talent for taking deep pleasure in common things. "To sit in idleness over a good fire in a well proportioned room is a luxurious sensation," she said of a "very quiet evening" with neighbors. "Sometimes we talked & sometimes we were quite silent." Her brother James's wife Mary was there for the same evening, and "found it dull,"[289] but for Austen, even as lively as she was, a quiet, lovely fire was a sumptuous thing. In London with Henry, in spite of being away from her sweet countryside, she could revel in "exquisite weather": "*I* enjoy it all over me, from top to toe, from right to left, Longitudinally, Perpendicularly, Diagonally."[290]

As a young woman, Austen could dance all night at a ball, provided she had enough partners. That gives me a picture of her lively self, and I like to think, ball or not, she continued to dance. Her spirit lilted, her heart was engrossed in the world around her.

Don't take yourself so seriously.

Austen surely thought seriously about the world, but she was never austere or somber, particularly in regard to herself. She was no pedantic, dreary Mary Bennet. Her letters are full of small jokes at her own expense. Away from home she begged to be remembered "to Everybody who does not enquire after me."[291] Trying to get to London (that "Scene of Dissipation & Vice"[292]) to visit friends, afraid she would find them away, she joked about being lured into the oldest profession, saying, "I should inevitably fall a Sacrifice to the arts of some fat Woman who would make me drunk with Small Beer."[293] (She was likely referencing *The Harlot's Progress* by painter William Hogarth, which shows an innocent country girl being led astray by the mistress of a brothel.[294]) When reading Austen, if ever unsure about how to interpret her, it's generally safe to assume there was a smile playing at the corners of her mouth.

Her family and friends would have expected this. No doubt, many of them shared her gift, to one degree or another, and her humor had been developed and encouraged at home. Mrs. Knight, her brother Edward's adoptive mother, suggested that Jane might marry Reverend Papillon, the rector of Chawton, and this became for years a running family joke. Jane said, out of her gratitude to Mrs. Knight, "I *will* marry Mr Papillon, whatever may be his reluctance or my own.—I owe her much more than such a trifling sacrifice."[295] Her friends would expect jokes at their expense as well. She teased Martha Lloyd about carrying on in an unseemly fashion with another clergyman, the married and decades-older Dr. Mant. I'm sure these are just small examples of what would have been commonplace for the Austen family. For them, to write even something simple like a family letter meant injecting levity into the quotidian stuff of life. It's a shame none of Cassandra's letters remain; Jane thought them more entertaining than her own.

Don't be a brooding genius.

No doubt Austen was a genius, though it's doubtful she would have ever thought in those terms, or ranked herself so highly. Hers was not the kind of intellect that required brooding drama or desperate depression. She could bring a light heart even to her work—in so many ways her work grew out of that lightness, required it to thrive. When she talked about her writing with family or friends (even with her nieces and nephews), she did not present herself as one who felt she deserved an elevated position or who demanded homage. You get the sense that she valued their frank assessments of her work, though she hoped those frank words contained praise. She didn't see herself as infallible; writing to Cassandra about trying to get her hands on a new novel, she confessed: "I . . . am always half afraid of finding a clever novel too clever—& of finding my own story & my own people all forestalled."[296] But she didn't agonize over those fears.

One of my favorite lines is in a letter to her niece Anna, where she is offering constructive criticism on Anna's novel—a novel which was later, regrettably, thrown into the fire after Jane died:

> *Devereux Forester's being ruined by his Vanity is extremely good; but I wish you would not let him plunge into a "vortex of Dissipation". I do not object to the Thing, but I cannot bear the expression;—it is such thorough novel slang—and so old, that I dare say Adam met with it in the first novel he opened.*[297]

There is witty Jane as loving critic and uncompromising writer, hoping Anna would be able to laugh at the weaknesses in her own work the same way her Aunt Jane did.

Cry, then laugh. Or maybe just laugh.

Austen would use her laughter as a balm, as she did with her illness, or when she wrote about her "tears flow[ing] . . . at the melancholy idea"[298] of Tom Lefroy leaving town. There certainly were difficulties and likely even depressions in her life, times she was unable to be so bright. We have little record of those, but we know that when possible, she would have directed her heart back to the humor where it was most at home. When Martha had her heart broken by a mysterious Mr. W., Jane hoped after she had recovered a little that she would "be able to jest openly about"[299] him—as though laughter was an invaluable part of the healing process.

Even smaller things, that for most of us would only annoy us and lead to complaint, Jane approached with humor. She told Cassandra, "I will not say that your Mulberry trees are dead, but I am afraid they are not alive."[300] Of a bothersome leak in their Southampton home, she wrote, "Could my Ideas flow as fast as the rain in the Storecloset, it would be charming. . . . The contest between us & the Closet has now ended in our defeat; I have been obliged to move almost everything out of it, & leave it to splash itself as it likes."[301] I'm sure Jane wasn't immune to irascibility, but it wasn't where her heart lived.

Be gentle.

It's true that humor (or sarcasm) is often just a way of dressing up meanness, and Austen could veer into cruelty. She said of a new washing woman, "It does not look as if anything she touched would ever be clean."[302] And she joked about a painter from the castle in Southampton, "I suppose whenever the Walls want no touching up, he is employed about my Lady's face."[303] These are comparatively soft for Austen; but occasionally she crossed into malice. She would have been well aware of this. When she wrote her evening prayers, with their contrition over wrongs done to others, perhaps she had this weakness in mind. Her favorite study was not art or music, but people. There was always something to laugh at there, some inconsistency or vulnerability to capture. She had the lively sharpness of Elizabeth Bennet rather than the quiet goodness of Lizzy's sister Jane. It's the reason she captured human nature with all its quirks, why we still see fundamental truths in her characters today. Because she struggled against this, she never gave herself over to it entirely, nor would she approve of those whose sole joy is at the expense of others, who find it impossible to laugh without maiming someone else in the process.

Love silence.

Austen did not require constant entertainment. In a world much quieter than our own, she still craved occasional silence—those evenings sitting by the fire. In *Persuasion,* she writes of the countryside around Lyme, and of Charmouth's "sweet retired bay, backed by dark cliffs, where fragments of low rock among the sands make it the happiest spot for watching the flow of the tide, for sitting in unwearied contemplation."[304] Austen had no doubt sat in that very spot during family trips to the sea, enjoying her own "unwearied contemplation." In our frenetic world, perhaps we've lost the value of silence and centeredness—the self-knowledge that kind of reflection can provide. We may associate Austen most with lively repartee, but she was just as happy alone, and needed time apart to be fully herself. I think her joy was fed in large part by the peace she found in stillness, especially in the beauty of being outside.

Take joy.

Jane Austen could not be apathetic or dull. Life never bored her. She approached it with hearty, unfaltering vigor, with a temperament disposed to fully experiencing all that was passing around her, with a true capacity for contentment. Her great energy effervesced into her novels, giving them the lightness, the liveliness we love. Only *her* heart and mind could have given us the stories she did. Her spirit was indomitable. She would find amusement, she would take joy.

If I could inherit one thing from Austen, I would harness a bit of her energy and delight—to take deep pleasure in small things, to meet life with animated expectation, and above all—always—to laugh.

Austen's Ethos

As I've written about Austen, several themes continue to come back to me. They've surfaced throughout the book, but, at the risk of redundancy, may bear repeating, because in so many ways I think they capture her heart. They were lessons her heroines knew, or came to know through the course of the stories, and may in fact be the central, overarching lessons she would want to pass on to us today. They're also lessons that, because of the two centuries that separate us from Austen, we may be less likely to take away from her light stories.

We cherish Austen's laughter, but may not immediately recognize that it was a laughter that grew out of the firmest of moral foundations. Ironically, without her exacting standards, there would have been little at all to laugh at. As C. S. Lewis pointed out in his essay on Austen[305], if everything had been acceptable to her, there would have been nothing ridiculous, nothing beyond the pale, none of the spark of humor that is created in the friction between what *is* and what *ought to be*. In other words, in a world in which greed is morally acceptable, *Sense and Sensibility*'s avaricious John and Fanny Dashwood cease to be funny.

I'm again struck with the remarkable balance Austen achieved. She cared about virtue without being tedious about it. She laughed at the world not because she was careless—after all, she would think and pray and reason along with that laughter—but the laughter made everything easier. Still, on sober subjects, she could be quite serious.

Question the acceptable.

Austen never took things at face value. For her, something was never acceptable just because it was accepted. It had to have some greater worth than mere popularity. In other words, society's approval of something didn't count for that much with her. As much as we have a starched and rigid notion of eighteenth century life, there were many things prevalent then that Austen never would have condoned. All the chasing after money, all the arrogance and hauteur that went along with having a place in society, all the people who were deemed important but were utterly thoughtless—all these things were eminently acceptable in the world around her but ridiculous to Austen. She played in and explored that region between what was allowed and what was morally right.

Austen's heroines could have married simply for money as Willoughby did, been stingy and spiteful like Fanny Dashwood, been haughty like *Pride and Prejudice*'s Lady Catherine de Bourgh, and still would have been welcome, even elevated, members of society. But Austen required something more of them. Austen required them to live up to a stricter code. She would remind us that following along with what everyone else finds acceptable is not necessarily the most rewarding or sensible path.

In our era we are eminently comfortable with questioning, but we do so with an aim that is the opposite of Austen's. We tend to question standards with a view to relaxing them; we may bristle at the thought of society imposing any sort of rule whatsoever, or at the very thought of making moral judgments. Austen comes at things from another angle, wondering if the accepted standards are high enough. If aspects of our own society trouble us—perhaps the same sorts of things that troubled Austen, like greed, pride, and thoughtlessness—she would have us explore what ought to be the higher ideal, the best way.

Find your inner guide.

Austen's characters, and Austen herself, all acted with a consciousness—an awareness—of a guide for good and bad, right and wrong. It was conscience, but also more than that. Austen's guide was a combination of the societal standards of the time along with her sincere Christian faith, which taught her that humility and kindness were to be valued more than pride and selfishness, that the pursuit of money was not life's highest aim, and that one of the goals of life was to continually be forging one's character, learning from mistakes and becoming better as a result. For Austen, the substance of a heart (or soul) was more important than property or place in society, and one could not really be happy without true goodness. All through Austen's writing, there is this sense of guidance, of unbending principles that touch not only great acts and grand gestures but also daily conduct.

Austen's faith formed and shaped her moral intuition. It challenged her to live up to a higher standard, the way she challenged her characters to do the same. We all know the voice of conscience, the still, small calling to do the right thing. Austen might encourage us to think through the sources that inform our own inner guide. Ultimately, what is it that challenges us to be better? If Austen equated goodness with happiness, we may be tempted to turn that equation on its head, to make happiness the supreme good and to justify anything in the name of getting there. For Austen, that would represent a great moral poverty. So what do we mean by *good*? Do we still believe that virtue can lead to happiness? Austen would have ready answers; ours may need to be explored.

Think for yourself.

Not only does Austen want us to think, to reason, but she wants us to stand by our own judgments, particularly our moral judgments. She and her characters embody the kind of fearless independence that holds firm to beliefs, no matter what. Once they know what is right, they do it at any cost and won't be bullied otherwise.

One of Austen's best examples of this is timid Fanny Price in *Mansfield Park*. In my opinion, Fanny can be a difficult character to like because she has none of Lizzy's spirit—she has only goodness and strength of character. C. S. Lewis calls her "insipid," and I have to agree. Henry Crawford—the same Henry Crawford who eventually seduces Maria Bertram (or perhaps it was the other way around)—wants to marry Fanny, but Fanny is rightfully unsure of his character. To fully appreciate Fanny's situation, you have to understand that she is poor. She's been living with her rich aunt and uncle at their grand estate, rescued from her family's hovel in Portsmouth and given a precious education. She owes everything to them. The match with Henry is particularly eligible for her, and both her cousin Edmund, whom she loves, and her uncle—a man who expects to be obeyed—urge the match. Her uncle fiercely accuses her of being "self-willed, obstinate, selfish, and ungrateful"[306] by refusing to give Henry her consent. But Fanny knows in her heart the match with Henry could never be right. She sees deep flaws in his character that the others miss. She knew "how wretched and how unpardonable, how hopeless and how wicked it was, to marry without affection."[307] She won't allow herself to be forced into something, even by those who know her best and believe they have her sincere interests at heart.

As much as I have a difficult time loving Fanny, I have no doubt that Austen would want us to emulate her strength. She would want us to rely on our own conclusions, even when they may be different from those of the world around us and even those closest to us. She would never want us to give in to pressure exerted on behalf of something wrong, or wrong for us, even by those who love us.

Be undeceived.

As we've seen and as Lewis stresses in his essay, Austen's primary hope for many of her characters is that they will be undeceived as to their own motivations and actions, that they will truly know themselves and thus be able to set themselves right. All of this talk about questioning things and examining moral standards is, in Austen's world, not meant with the least kind of revolutionary tone or missionary zeal. She doesn't aim for her characters to set about changing the world or reforming the people around them—perhaps because that would have been as indecorous as impossible. Elizabeth Bennet may stand up to Lady Catherine de Bourgh, may anger her, which is about as revolutionary as Austen gets, but Elizabeth's goal was not to influence Lady Catherine for the better. (Although perhaps ultimately she did.) When given the opportunity, Austen's characters speak truth without hedging, but none of them are on a mission, except as it pertains to themselves and their own lives. Their primary goal—which we may miss in our haste to get to the happy ending—is not to catch a husband, but to be virtuous, blameless. With virtue, Austen knew they would have joy.

She would want that joy for us, the joy that comes from self-knowledge and surety, from strength of character. And centuries later, she might be able to help us get there.

Acknowledgments

This book would not exist without my editor, Lara Asher, who first conceived it. I'm incredibly grateful that she gave me this opportunity, and for her expert guidance. It takes much more than words to produce and sell a book, and I am indebted to Sheryl Kober for her beautiful design work and to Kristen Mellitt for shepherding this project through. I'm so glad we were able to include Dave Grant's illustrations—what a gift. My agent Andrea Heinecke at Alive Communications makes it possible for me to do the work I love.

Writing while living with chronic Lyme disease presents challenges. My parents provide unending, incalculable amounts of love and support; I couldn't have done this without them. I'm thankful beyond words for my doctor, Leila Zackrison, whose care made this project possible, and who has helped me believe in the potential of a healthy future.

Like Austen, I'm blessed with a small group of dear friends who give my life so much richness. Catherine Claire Larson walked through this project with me with generous encouragement and faith. Taylor Holt Wlodarczak is my daily companion through the mess of Lyme. Her laughter and empathy make the journey so much easier to bear. Sweet Brenda Hoffman, Diane Gray, and Beth McElroy are further afield but equally cherished. A large group prayed for me throughout this journey; I'm so thankful for them, for their prayers, and for the innumerable gifts God has given along the way.

Endnotes

1 Letters, 26.
2 Letters, 203.
3 P&P, 273 (III, XIV).
4 FR, 50.
5 Letters, 217.
6 FR, 104.
7 FR, 144.
8 Letters, 175.
9 *Susan,* or *Northanger Abbey,* pokes fun at Gothic romances. Crosby & Co. made a lot of money publishing Gothic romances, which may be why they decided not to publish it.
10 S&S, 38 (I, IV).
11 Ibid.
12 Letters, 277.
13 Letters, 201.
14 Letters, 182.
15 Letters, 287.
16 P&P, 33 (I, IX).
17 P&P, 177 (II, XVIII).
18 P&P, 235 (III, VIII).
19 Letters, 340.
20 P, 160 (II, IX).
21 S&S, 258 (II, I).
22 S&S, 256 (II, I).
23 S&S, 500 (III, II).
24 Letters, 74–75.
25 Letters, 31.
26 P&P, 58 (I, XVI).
27 P&P, 170 (II, XVI).
28 C, 247.
29 Letters, xiii.
30 Letters, 17.
31 E, 288 (III, VII).
32 E, 291 (III, VII).

33 E, 294–96 (III, VII).
34 P&P, 159 (II, XIII).
35 C, 248.
36 NA, 146 (II, X).
37 NA, 146 (II, IX).
38 NA, 147 (II, X).
39 Ibid.
40 Letters, 38.
41 P&P, 278 (III, XV).
42 Letters, 1.
43 Ibid.
44 Letters, 2.
45 Letters, 3–4.
46 Letters, 2.
47 Letters, 4.
48 P&P, 211 (III, IV).
49 Ibid.
50 P&P, 7 (I, III).
51 P&P, 19 (I, VI).
52 P&P, 13 (I, V).
53 P&P, 69 (I, XVIII).
54 C, 247.
55 P&P, 156 (II, XIII).
56 P&P, 159 (II, XIII).
57 FR, 106.
58 Letters, 216.
59 Letters, 285.
60 P, 26–27 (I, IV).
61 P, 28 (I, IV).
62 P, 157 (II, IX).
63 S&S, 36–38 (I, IV).
64 S&S, 500 (III, II).
65 P&P, 248 (III, X).
66 P, 194 (II, XI).
67 NA, 180 (II, XV).
68 P, 12 (I, I).
69 S&S, 70–72 (I, VIII).
70 Letters, 279.

71 Letters, 280.
72 Ibid.
73 Letters, 286.
74 Letters, 330.
75 P&P, 237 (III, VIII).
76 MP, 353 (III, XVI).
77 S&S, 30 (I, III).
78 S&S, 644 (III, X).
79 S&S, 706 (III, XIV).
80 Letters, 57.
81 Letters, 29.
82 Letters, 226.
83 Letters, 303.
84 Letters, 301.
85 Letters, 237.
86 Letters, 198.
87 Letters, 121.
88 P&P, 9 (I, IV).
89 P&P, 6 (I, III).
90 P, 26 (I, IV).
91 S&S 36, (I, IV).
92 MP, 35 (I, V).
93 P&P, 16 (I, VI).
94 Letters, 286.
95 P, 130–31 (II, V).
96 MP, 370 (III, XVII).
97 S&S, 106, (I, XI).
98 Letters, 286.
99 S&S, 486–48 (III, I).
100 S&S, 488 (III, I).
101 E, 303 (III, IX).
102 E, 338 (III, XIII).
103 Letters, 329.
104 Letters, 332.
105 Letters, 280.
106 Letters, 4.
107 FR, 143.
108 Letters, 215.

109 FR, 101.
110 Claire Tomalin, *Jane Austen: A Life* (New York: Vintage, 1999), 125.
111 Memoir, 70.
112 Letters, 5.
113 Letters, 281.
114 S&S, 344 (II, VII).
115 S&S, 324 (II, VI).
116 S&S, 336–38 (II, VII).
117 S&S, 342 (II, VII).
118 S&S, 198 (I, XIX).
119 S&S, 564 (III, VI).
120 Ibid.
121 S&S, 580 (III, VII).
122 S&S, 644 (III, X).
123 S&S, 342 (II, VII).
124 S&S, 252 (I, XXII).
125 S&S, 258 (II, I).
126 S&S, 252 (I, XXII).
127 S&S, 258 (II, I).
128 S&S, 482–84 (III, I).
129 S&S, 486 (III, I).
130 S&S, 488–90 (III, I).
131 S&S, 342 (II, VII).
132 S&S, 486, 490 (III, I).
133 P, 85 (I, XII).
134 P, 87 (I, XII).
135 P, 118 (II, IV).
136 P, 155 (II, IX).
137 S&S, 652–54 (III, XI).
138 P&P, 210 (III, IV).
139 NA, 145 (II, IX).
140 P, 61 (I, VIII)
141 P&P, 286 (III, XVII).
142 Letters, 286.
143 P&P, 93 (I, XXII).
144 Ibid.
145 P&P, 94 (I, XXII).
146 FR, 137–38.

147 P&P, 16 (I, VI).
148 FR, 70.
149 Letters, 146–49.
150 NA, 186 (II, XVI).
151 NA, 180 (II, XV).
152 P, 202 (II, XII).
153 S&S, 706 (III, XIV).
154 MP, 372 (III, XVII).
155 Letters, 335.
156 P, 78 (I, X).
157 P&P, 297 (III, XIX).
158 P&P, 180 (II, XIX).
159 Ibid.
160 P&P, 94 (I, XXII).
161 Letters, 241.
162 Letters, 168.
163 Letters, 125.
164 Letters, 344.
165 Letters, 102.
166 Letters, 264.
167 Letters, 30.
168 Ibid.
169 Letters, 97.
170 Letters, 267.
171 Letters, 228.
172 Letters, 186.
173 Letters, 121.
174 Letters, 225.
175 Letters, 116.
176 Letters, 148.
177 Letters, 78.
178 Letters, 146.
179 Letters, 148.
180 Letters, 150.
181 FR, 267.
182 Letters, 33.
183 P, 11 (I, I).
184 Letters, 29.

185 Letters, 287.
186 Letters, 64.
187 Letters, 250.
188 Letters, 265.
189 Letters, 39.
190 Letters, 146–47.
191 Letters, 139.
192 Ibid.
193 Letters, 28.
194 Letters, 217.
195 I Timothy 6:10, King James Version.
196 Letters, 287.
197 Letters, 252.
198 Letters, 281.
199 FR, 163.
200 S&S, 6 (I, I).
201 Ibid.
202 Ibid.
203 S&S, 14 (I, II).
204 S&S, 15 (I, II).
205 S&S, 20 (I, II).
206 Memoir, 140.
207 Letters, 133.
208 Letters, 138.
209 Letters, 30.
210 Letters, 3.
211 FR, 188.
212 Letters, 218.
213 Letters, 231.
214 *The Critical Review,* February 1812, as quoted in FR, 189.
215 FR, 195.
216 FR, 196.
217 Letters, 250.
218 Letters, 221.
219 Letters, 335.
220 *Famous Reviews,* ed. R. Brimley Johnson, Project Gutenberg, ebook published 2004, Kindle location 3,335–45.
221 Letters, 250.

222 Memoir, 92.
223 Letters, 296.
224 Letters, 306.
225 Letters, 307.
226 Letters, 312.
227 Letters, 145.
228 Letters, 110.
229 Letters, 312.
230 FR, 176–77.
231 Letters, 15.
232 Letters, 165.
233 Letters, 144.
234 Letters, 328–29.
235 Letters, 323.
236 Letters, 327
237 Letters, 285.
238 Letters, 249.
239 E, 69 (I, X).
240 Letters, 140.
241 Letters, 6.
242 Letters, 336.
243 Letters, 142.
244 Letters, 119.
245 Letters, 251.
246 Letters, 201.
247 Letters, 323.
248 Letters, 275.
249 Letters, 321.
250 Letters, 332.
251 Letters, 53.
252 Letters, 329.
253 Letters, 157.
254 E, 68–69 (I, X).
255 FR, 128.
256 Letters, 85.
257 Letters, 88.
258 Letters, 86.
259 C, 238.

260 Letters, 97.
261 Letters, 29–30.
262 Letters, 320.
263 Letters, 323.
264 Letters, 335–36.
265 Letters, 338.
266 Letters, 231.
267 Letters, 336.
268 Letters, 326.
269 Ibid.
270 Letters, 329.
271 Letters, 320.
272 Letters, 340.
273 Letters, 327.
274 Letters, 333.
275 P, 125 (II, V).
276 Letters, 338.
277 Letters, 342.
278 Letters, 341.
279 Ibid.
280 Letters, 340.
281 Letters, 341.
282 FR, 251.
283 Letters, 344.
284 Sir Walter Scott's journal, March 14, 1826, available online at www.readbookonline.net/read/5144/17465/.
285 Letters, 347.
286 Letters, 38.
287 Letters, 16.
288 Letters, 128.
289 Letters, 56.
290 Letters, 303.
291 Letters, 8.
292 Letters, 5.
293 Letters, 12.
294 Letters, 359.
295 Letters, 156.
296 Letters, 186.

297 Letters, 277.
298 Letters, 4.
299 Letters, 17.
300 Letters, 190.
301 Letters, 169.
302 Letters, 18.
303 Letters, 119.
304 P, 80 (I, XI).
305 C. S. Lewis, *Selected Literary Essays,* edited by Walter Hooper (Cambridge: Cambridge University Press, 1969), 175–86.
306 MP, 250 (III, I).
307 MP, 254 (III, I).